THE **MINI** ROUGH GUIDE TO
ATHENS

ROUGH GUIDES

YOUR TAILOR-MADE TRIP
STARTS HERE

Tailor-made trips and unique adventures crafted by local experts

HOW ROUGHGUIDES.COM/TRIPS WORKS

STEP 1

Pick your dream destination, tell us what you want and submit an enquiry.

STEP 2

Fill in a short form to tell your local expert about your dream trip and preferences.

STEP 3

Our local expert will craft your tailor-made itinerary. You'll be able to tweak and refine it until you're completely satisfied.

STEP 4

Book online with ease, pack your bags and enjoy the trip! Our local expert will be on hand 24/7 while you're on the road.

PLAN AND BOOK YOUR TRIP AT
ROUGHGUIDES.COM/TRIPS

HOW TO DOWNLOAD
YOUR FREE EBOOK

1. Visit **www.roughguides.com/
   free-ebook** or scan the **QR
   code** opposite

2. Enter the code **athens808**

3. Follow the simple step-by-step
   instructions

For troubleshooting contact: mail@roughguides.com

10 THINGS NOT TO MISS

1. **ACROPOLIS MUSEUM**
   A splendid repository for the antiquities of the Acropolis, with space for the Elgin Marbles. See page 38.

2. **BENAKI MUSEUM PIREÓS ANNEXE**
   Multiple changing exhibits, always top-notch. See page 53.

3. **THE GOULANDRIS MUSEUM OF CONTEMPORARY ART**
   State-of-the-art gallery featuring most major figures in painting and sculpture since the 1890s through to the present day. A must-see cultural delight for all ages. See page 64.

4. **THE NATIONAL ARCHAEOLOGICAL MUSEUM**
   Admire Kouros statues at the National Archaeological Museum. See page 55.

5. **THE ACROPOLIS**
   Topped by one of the world's greatest cultural monuments, the Parthenon, this is the rock around which ancient Athens was founded. See page 29.

6. **PLÁKA**
   A maze of narrow streets lined with restaurants, museums and Neoclassical mansions. See page 41.

7. **THE ATHENS AND EPIDAUROS FESTIVAL**
   Especially on a moonlit night, a performance at Herodes Atticus or Epidaurus is magical. See page 83.

8. **DELPHI**
   Make an excursion to the ancient home of the Delphic oracle. See page 78.

9. **NÁVPLIO**
   This old port town makes an ideal base for exploring the Argolid. See page 77.

10. **THE BYZANTINE AND CHRISTIAN MUSEUM**
    Cutting-edge museology showcases unexpected artefacts. See page 63.

A PERFECT TOUR

Day 1

Acropolis and around. Get to the Acropolis before the crowds, walking up from Acropolis metro station along pedestrianised Dionysíou Areopagítou and perhaps taking in the Theatre of Dionysos en route. Descend via Pláka, stopping at a low-key local museum such as the Kanellopoulos. Have lunch around Monastiráki, perhaps at Kapnikarea (with live music). Time it so that you arrive at the New Acropolis Museum late in the afternoon, with the Parthenon catching the setting sun while you admire the pediments on the top floor. Treat yourself to an upmarket supper at Mani-Mani in Makrygiánni.

Day 2

Kolonáki and Pangráti museums. From Evangelismós metro station, the Benaki Museum and the Byzantine and Christian Museum are just a short walk away, both enhanced by temporary exhibitions. After lunch on or near Platía Proskópon, across busy Vassiléos Konstandínou in the up-and-coming Pangráti neighbourhood, take in the magnificent collection at the Goulandris Museum of Contemporary Art, with Pangráti again a likely destination for dinner afterwards.

Day 3

Psyrrí and Thisío. From Thisío métro station, stroll to the Kerameikos ancient site, and then marvel at the exhibits in the Benaki Museum of Islamic Art in adjacent Psyrrí before lunch at Nikitas. For some contemporary art or photography, head along to a choice of temporary exhibitions at the Benaki Pireós 138 Annexe (both closed Mon–Wed, Pireós 138 all Aug). On Fri/Sat there's late opening at Pireós 138 so you can linger. Afterwards, a pleasant walk takes you to Petrálona, the Pláka or Makrygiánni for dinner.

OF **ATHENS**

Day 4

Retail therapy. On Sunday you'll find the Monastiráki flea
market in full swing. Weekdays, continue north through the
central bazaar to the picturesque Varvákios food hall; lunch is
nearby at Thanasis, Ta Karamanlidika tou Fani or Klimataria.
Walk south to the Hephaisteion temple, the Stoa of Attalos
and the ancient Agora, and then take in the Jewish Museum
in Pláka plus the nearby Temple of Olympian Zeus. After
dinner, between May and September, enjoy a film at an
outdoor cinema in Petrálona, Pláka or Thisío districts.

Day 5

Delphi. Pick up a hire car and head west to ancient Delphi;
you'll need to stay overnight in Aráhova, modern Delfí
village or Galaxídi on the Corinth Gulf for a relaxed visit to
both the sprawling site and the museum.

Day 6

Peloponnese. The following day, use the spectacular
Río-Andírrio bridge, or the much cheaper ferry, to cross to
the Corinth Gulf's south coast. Take in ancient Corinth and
Mycenae en route to Návplio, where you can stay overnight.

Day 7

National Museum and Soúnio. Visit the National
Archaeological Museum in Athens and catch the sunset at
Soúnio's Poseidon Temple after a trip to ancient Epidauros.

Day 8

Argo-Saronic Gulf. Explore the Argo-Saronic islands:
choose Égina for Aphaia Temple and Paleohóra, or Ýdra for
its car-free harbour and coastal hike.

CONTENTS

OVERVIEW

A demographic shift

Athens is by far the biggest city in Greece, although it is currently experiencing population decline. The central boroughs and surrounding suburbs are now home to 3.17 million people.

Mention the name Athens, and almost everyone will have some preconceived ideas about the city. Socrates painted a verbal picture in the 4th century BC; Pausanias followed suit in the Roman era. 19th-century travellers gave it an air of romance. During the 1960s, the Greek film industry added its own spin with such movies as *Never on Sunday* and *The Red Lanterns*, and schoolchildren still learn about the twelve great gods of ancient Greece.

This fair-sized (at least one hundred and fifty thousand) ancient city set on and around a dramatic hill of rock – the Acropolis – became the cradle of Western civilisation. During its 5th- and 4th-century BC heyday, Athenians were highly sophisticated in their thoughts and actions, their tastes and fashions. They left an enduring legacy of concepts and ideas for humankind, but also a remarkable number of buildings and artefacts that tell us about their lives. The remains of the buildings atop and around the Acropolis are instantly recognisable, and hundreds of statues, along with household pottery, jewellery and tools exert a fascination on anyone who enjoys exploring the past.

THE MODERN CAPITAL

The city of Athens is more than a sum of these ancient parts. After Constantinople became the capital of the eastern Roman Empire in 330 AD, Athens gradually shrank to little more than a village, only to rise phoenix-like from the ashes after 1834, the year it was designated

Bustling Monastiráki Square with the Acropolis and the Tzisdarákis mosque in the background

capital of the modern Greek state. Neoclassical design was fashionable across Europe during the mid-19th century, and the impressive buildings then constructed in Athens could be seen beside their prototypes. The elegant simplicity of the Parliament (originally the royal palace), the graceful facade of the University, and decoration on the Academy all hark back to ancient examples. In 1923, following the collapse of the Ottoman Empire and Greece's ultimately repelled invasion of Anatolia, Greece and republican Turkey agreed on a population exchange based on religious grounds which brought to Greece more than one million Orthodox Christians, resident in Asia Minor since antiquity. Athens strained to accommodate many of them in the first hastily erected suburbs around the central area. The result is that much of Athens is overbuilt, with congested, narrow streets and a shortage of green space and parking. The post-World War II policy of *andiparohí* also radically changed the look of the city, giving rise to urban planning challenges that still exist today (see page 27).

ORIENTATION

Since the millennium, the heart of Athens, the central, 19th-century triangular grid defined by Sýndagma (Sýntagma) and Omónia squares and the Kerameikos archaeological site, has been rejuvenated with pedestrianised streets, carefully renovated Neoclassical buildings and attractive lighting. Just beyond, the districts of Monastiráki and Pláka immediately south, and the Acropolis above these, contain many of the most interesting places to see.

A still-expanding metró system provides efficient service along three main lines and out to the easterly airport, which can also be reached by a suburban rail line from the city's main train station, Stathmós Laríssis. Trams run south from Néos Kósmos to the seaside suburbs of Glyfáda and Néo Fáliro. The Attikí Odós toll ring-road through northern Athens, with its spur around Mt Ymittós, allows you to drive easily between different parts of Athens, and to bypass the centre if travelling between the airport and the Peloponnese or Delphi. If you are heading for the islands, ferries, hydrofoils and catamarans fan out from the ports of Piraeus, Lávrio and Rafína.

ATHENIAN WAY OF LIFE

Athens is a city to be enjoyed outdoors. Every district has its own small, leafy squares with cafés and tavernas where people gather for a drink or meal. Although there are now numerous foreign and nouvelle-Greek-cuisine restaurants, traditional, good-value tavernas are still popular, especially in these straitened times.

Tradition still plays an important part in daily life. The family forms the backbone of Greek society and filial ties are strong. Although crêches are increasingly used by working parents, children still play safely in the streets with *giagiá* (grandma) keeping a watchful eye; new babies are proudly shown to the world during the evening *vólta* (stroll).

The Orthodox Church – long the symbolic unifier of the Greek diaspora, and constitutionally an established religion – has seen its influence wane considerably in recent decades. Religious observance remains strongest among older women, who still stop in the nearest church to reverence an icon or light a candle for the living or the dead.

CRITICAL TIMES

Since joining the European Community in 1981, Greece has received huge sums in aid for upgrading infrastructure (especially transport and telecoms) throughout the country, which came in handy when Athens staged the Olympic Games for the second time in 2004. However, it is now evident that Greece's accession to the euro in 2002 was helped along using doctored accounts, with an ensuing economic disaster. Greece has hovered on the brink of default in paying off a truly colossal debt to foreign banks since early 2010. In a 2015 referendum, the majority of Greeks voted not to accept a bailout tied to strict austerity measures, resulting in growing fears of a Greek exit from the eurozone (dubbed 'Grexit'). In 2016, a new compromise was reached: lenders agreed to restructure Greece's debts on the condition that Greece remained committed to a series of economic reforms. In late 2018 it was announced that Greece had finally exited 'special' supervisory measures.

Changing of the Guard

HISTORY AND CULTURE

In ancient Greek mythology, Athens was named following a contest between Athena, Goddess of wisdom, and Poseidon, God of the sea. Both coveted the city, so it was agreed that whoever produced the more useful gift for mortals would win. Legendary half-human, half-serpent king of Athens, Kekrops, acted as arbiter.

First Poseidon struck the rock of the Acropolis with his mighty trident and brought saltwater gushing forth. Then it was Athena's turn. She conjured an olive tree, which proved more useful and valuable. Thus, she became the city's special protector.

ANCIENT CITY-STATE

The real story of the city-state of Athens is just as fascinating. The earliest Athenian settlement, dating from around 3000 BC, was built atop the Acropolis. During the late Bronze Age, also known as the Mycenaean era after King Agamemnon's famous Argolid city, a large palace was erected there too. For several centuries, the Mycenaeans dominated the eastern Mediterranean and Aegean. A long series of conflicts, however, including the legendary siege of Troy, weakened their militaristic civilisation.

The city-state of Athens came to occupy the entire Attic peninsula 50km (31 miles) south to Cape Sounion, northeast to the Rhamnous fortress and temple, and west to Megara, a total of 3,885 sq km (1,500 sq miles). This extensive territory included some highly advantageous natural resources. The broad Mesogeia plain was in antiquity and remains today a productive farming area, able to support the growing population. The Laurio (today Lávrio) mines near Sounion yielded silver; the mountains of Ymittós and Pendéli provided marble for building; and both

Pireás and Pórto Ráfti were large natural harbours – factors critical to Athenian strength.

TOWARDS DEMOCRACY

Perhaps because of water shortages, Athens developed later than other city-states, but by the late 7th century BC was a major power. The first steps towards democracy were taken early in the 6th century BC under Solon, an Athenian merchant and poet appointed to reform the constitution. He cancelled all debts for which land or liberty could be forfeited and established a new council *(boule)* of four hundred members to formulate proposals discussed in the full assembly of adult male citizens.

The Peisistratid tyrants held power between 561 and 510 BC, and under their rule, commerce and the arts flourished. Attiki's

Mosaic of Dionysos from a Roman villa, Corinth (2nd century CE)

(Attica's) wine and olive oil were shipped to Italy, Egypt and Asia Minor in beautiful black-figure pots; the first tragedies ever written were performed at the annual festival of the wine god, Dionysos; and standardised versions of Homer's works were set down.

Further constitutional and electoral reforms were made in 508 BC under Kleisthenes who created ten artificial tribes, each based on domicile rather than blood-ties and consisting of the same

THE ANCIENT GREEK PANTHEON

Following a May 2006 Athens court ruling, it is no longer illegal to worship the ancient Greek gods. Here's a summary of the main deities.

Zeus rules gods and mortals and controls the weather; his symbols are the eagle, thunder and the oak tree. **Hera** is Zeus' main, oft-betrayed wife, Patroness of Marriage and Motherhood. **Athena**, daughter of Zeus, is Goddess of Wisdom and Crafts, Guardian of War Heroes, and inventor of the loom and potter's wheel. **Apollo**, son of Zeus by the titaness Leto, was the Deity of Music, Healing, Prophecy and the Sun. His twin sister **Artemis** was Goddess of Hunting and the Moon, also Guardian of Animals and Young Virgins. **Hermes**, another son of Zeus, was the Gods' messenger, Escorter of Dead Souls and God of Commerce, Orators and Writers, as well as Protector of Flocks, Thieves and Travellers. **Ares**, God of War, another son of Zeus, was unpopular on Olympos and feared by mortals. Lame **Hephaistos**, God of Fire and Metallurgy, yet another sibling, was the divine blacksmith. He was married to **Aphrodite**, Goddess of Love, Beauty and Gardens. **Poseidon**, Zeus's brother, presided over seas, rivers and all creatures therein. **Hades**, another brother, ruled the kingdom of the dead – but also controlled all subterranean mineral wealth. **Demeter**, sister of Zeus, was Goddess of Agriculture and Protectress of Crops.

number of people from central city, coast and inland. These provided military support, elected officials, and sent representatives to a new council of five hundred members, which replaced Solon's four hundred-member council. However, all this co-existed with extensive recourse to slavery; captives brought from Thrace and Asia Minor worked the Laurio silver mines in particular.

THE PERSIAN WARS

During the 5th century BC, the Athenians twice stopped the great Persian Empire from invading from the east: in late summer of 490 BC, their army defeated a Persian force sent by Darius I on the plain of Marathon, just 43km (26 miles) northeast of Athens. According to legend, the soldier Pheidippides, who ran from Marathon to Athens, died of exhaustion and heat-stroke immediately after reporting the victory. His feat is commemorated in the 26-mile (43km) Olympic marathon.

Ten years later Darius I's son, Xerxes I, occupied Athens and burned the Acropolis, only to see his own fleet destroyed off the island of Salamis, opposite Piraeus, by the Athenian navy.

PELOPONNESIAN WAR, MACEDONIAN RULE

Following the Persian Wars, Athens and Sparta were the two most powerful Greek city-states. Each sought dominance, until their rivalry erupted in the long Peloponnesian War (431–404 BC), which ended in Athenian defeat. The repressive government installed by the Spartans in Athens was soon overthrown, and the Athenians joined Persia to defeat the Spartan navy in 394 BC. In 338 BC Athens and Thebes, now allied against the common threat of Macedonia under Philip II, were defeated at Chaironeia in Boeotia, northwest of Attica. Philip became the ruler of mainland Greece until his assassination, when he was succeeded by his son Alexander (later the Great). Their rule of Athens was benign, and despite strong resentment of Macedonian domination, the city flourished.

CLASSICAL, HELLENISTIC AND ROMAN PERIODS

The 157 years between the victory over the Persians at Salamis in 480 BC and the death of Alexander the Great in 323 BC were times of extraordinary intellectual and cultural activity for Athens.

The great philosophers Sokrates (Socrates), Plato and Aristotle lived during this period, as did the playwrights Aristophanes and Sophokles, the historians Herodotos (Herodotus) and Thukydides (Thucydides), the sculptors Pheidias and Praxiteles, and the statesman Perikles (Pericles). The work of these and many other gifted men laid the groundwork for much of European civilisation. Many of the physical remains of this extraordinary flowering are concentrated on the Acropolis and in the centre of the ancient city, the Greek Agora.

The Romans patronised Athens after taking control of Greece in 146 BC, coming to the city to study. Julius Caesar had the Roman

Agora built just east of the Athenian Agora, and Hadrian (emperor 117–138 CE) commissioned the construction of the Library of Hadrian while completing the Olympian Zeus temple. In the 3rd century AD the Heruli, a Germanic tribe expelled from Scandinavia by the Danes, appeared in the Black Sea and continued south to wreak havoc in Greece. They burned Athens in 267 CE before moving on to sack Corinth, Sparta and Argos.

BYZANTINE EMPIRE

When the Roman emperor Constantine designated Byzantium (ie Constantinople – present-day İstanbul) as his new capital in 330 CE, the Empire became divided into eastern and western sectors. Rome was soon to fall to successive waves of invaders, but Constantinople thrived as the capital of the Byzantine Empire.

Carved flower detail, ancient Greek Agora

Athens continued to serve as a great educational and cultural centre until 529, when the Christian emperor Justinian I ordered that the Pagan philosophical Athenian Academy be closed. The Parthenon and other temples elsewhere had already been turned into churches in 435. But the demise of the school led to the city's decline into an unimportant provincial town.

In 1204 the Fourth Crusade sacked and occupied Constantinople, and in 1205 Athens was constituted as a Latin Catholic duchy under Burgundian, Catalan and Florentine over-lords, a status maintained until 1458.

OTTOMAN OCCUPATION

Byzantium fell in 1453 to Mehmet II and the Ottoman Turks, who reached Athens five years later. Many Albanian Christians, who

Mosaic in the Byzantine Museum

had served as mercenary troops for both the Byzantines and the Ottomans, moved to Athens and settled in Pláka.

The Ottomans made the Acropolis a Muslim precinct and the city acquired three purpose-built mosques – two of these still standing near the Roman Agora – as well as three hammams (bath-houses). The Ottomans also transformed a number of churches into mosques, including the Parthenon on the Acropolis, which acquired a minaret.

The Ottoman occupation of Athens was interrupted by war with the Venetians in 1687. Besieged on the Acropolis that autumn, the Ottomans were using the Parthenon for storing munitions. The Venetian commander, Francesco Morosini, brought his artillery, commanded by Swedish mercenary, Otto Wilhelm Königsmarck, to the hill of Pnyx. On 26 September, a shell scored a direct hit on the powder magazine, and the resulting explosion was devastating. Many defenders were killed, the Acropolis village was set alight, and the Parthenon suffered major damage for the first time.

The Turks surrendered and departed, the Venetians controlling the city until lack of men and a severe outbreak of plague forced them to leave by April 1688. The Athenians, who had welcomed the Christian Venetians but feared retribution after the inevitable Ottoman return, also fled Athens, leaving it uninhabited for three years. During the second period of Ottoman occupation, Pláka became the city's central commercial area.

Athenian houses at this time were normally built with a court-yard and, for both privacy and protection, they had few or no windows opening onto the narrow, haphazard streets. Most were two storeys high with the kitchen and storerooms on the ground floor; a wooden veranda, bedrooms, and the family common room were on the upper floor. Usually there were two knockers on the front door: one for servants and peasants; and another fancier, higher one for members of the family and upper-class visitors.

FIGHT FOR INDEPENDENCE

The Greek War of Independence began in the Peloponnese during
March 1821, and the Athenians expelled the Muslims from Athens
the following June, with much attendant massacre. Ottoman forces
returned in 1826 to besiege the city, capturing the Acropolis in
June 1827. The Greeks were obliged to sign a treaty turning Athens
over to the Ottomans, after which the Athenians retired to the
Argo-Saronic islands.

In 1830 the London Protocol was signed by Britain, France,
Russia and Turkey recognising Greece as an independent kingdom.
Otto of Bavaria was made King of Greece in 1832, and the last
Ottoman troops on the Acropolis finally surrendered in March
1833. In October 1834 Athens was officially declared the capital
of Greece.

At the time, the city was little more than a village, with a
population of about four thousand. During ancient times, the

population had reached 150,000, including slaves. Several grandiose plans were submitted, including one to build a large palace on the Acropolis. Instead Sýndagma (Constitution) Square was chosen as the site for the royal palace, now the Parliament building (*Vouli*). The overall city plan envisioned wide boulevards and squares within a triangle of three main streets, today Ermoú, Pireós and Stadíou. Ermoú runs from Sýndagma Square to the Kerameikos archaeological site; Pireós runs from Omónia Square past Kerameikos to the port of Piraeus; while Stadíou connects Omónia Square to Sýndagma Square. This 'commercial triangle' still defines the heart of Athens.

Strong German influence upon the designs of the buildings erected in post-independence Athens meant that the revival of Classical architecture in Greece was not based directly on examples of Classical antiquity, but on the Neoclassical style then popular in western Europe. The University of Athens on Panepistemíou Street, by Danish architect Hans Christian Hansen, is a fine example of this imported paradigm, and many mansions in this genre are scattered around Pláka and throughout the centre.

In 1862 King Otto was deposed and replaced by a young Danish prince, William, from the Glücksberg dynasty, who reigned successfully as George I from 1863 until his 1913 assassination in Thessaloníki.

EARLY 20TH CENTURY

Within just three years of becoming Greece's capital, the population of Athens had increased almost fourfold, and steady growth continued thereafter. A particularly large intake occurred during 1922–23, the result of a population exchange after Greece's reckless advance into Anatolia was routed by Turkish nationalist armies under Mustafa Kemal (later Atatürk). Approximately 390,000 Muslims left Greece for Turkey and almost 1,500,000

The 1896 Olympic Games

Greeks moved from western Anatolia and eastern Thrace to Greece. Many of these Orthodox Christian refugees settled in what are now affluent suburbs, nostalgically named after their abandoned homelands: Néa Iónia, Néa Smýrni, Néa Filadélfia (*néa* meaning new).

Between 1936 and 1941 Greece suffered under the military dictatorship of Ioannis Metaxas, who rejected Mussolini's demand that Greece give safe passage to the Italian army. During the winter of 1940–41 the Greek army stopped the Italian advance into Greek Îpiros (Epirus), a heroic accomplishment commemorated annually with a national holiday on 28 October.

In April 1941, Germany invaded Greece, defeating all Allied forces there by late May, with the country divided into Bulgarian, German and Italian occupation zones. Many Athenians starved during the following winter as all food was requisitioned by the occupiers. On 18 October 1944, British forces moved into Athens, encountering no opposition from the Germans, who had completed their withdrawal by 12 October.

The war left Greece utterly devastated. Communist and royalist partisans moved steadily towards a military confrontation as the United States, per the Truman Doctrine, supported the royalist central government. Three years of savage civil war ended in late 1949 with communist defeat. Political instability and repression persisted through the 1950s and early 1960s.

REIGN OF THE JUNTA

On 21 April 1967, the military – claiming to pre-empt a Communist takeover – seized power and tanks rolled through Athens. During the seven-year dictatorship of the junta, initially headed by Colonel George Papadopoulos (subsequently under a trio of generals), political parties were dissolved, the press was censored, and left-wing sympathisers were exiled or tortured and imprisoned.

THE LAW OF ANDIPAROHÍ

The law of Andiparohí, introduced in 1929, brought about a significant change to Athens' urban landscape. Widely implemented during the 1950s, it marked a departure from the city's gradual growth since the 1830s. Under this law, owners of a refugee shack or crumbling Neoclassical mansion alike could give their property to a developer, who would knock it down and erect a block of flats, with two or three allotted to the provider of the site in exchange. Both parties benefited: developers got free land while donating families received modern real estate. Unfortunately, Athens suffered aesthetically as monotonous concrete apartments spread everywhere until the 1990s, leaving little green space and few noteworthy new buildings.

THE WAY FORWARD

In 1981, the year that it entered the EC, Greece elected its first notionally socialist government under charismatic Andreas Papandreou and his PASOK party. Papandreou, while excluding the recently legalised Communist Party from government, finally recognised the leftist resistance organisations who had fought against the Axis World War II occupation. This was a major contribution to political stability, as was the 1989 destruction of all secret-police files. PASOK held power for most of the next three decades, before their support plummeted drastically as a result of the financial crisis and their acceptance of unpopular austerity measures – PASOK's George Papandreou resigned as prime minister in November 2011.

In January 2015, the radically leftist SYRIZA party, headed by Alexis Tsipras, finished first in parliamentary elections, forming a coalition government with the Eurosceptic Independent Greeks party (ANEL). Negotiations with Greece's creditors (the troika of the IMF, EU and ECB) broke down in late June, before a July referendum went massively against a third rescue package which would prolong severe austerity measures. Despite this, Tsipras caved into the troika and used late-summer elections to rid his government of dissidents. Improvement in economic conditions was excruciatingly slow, and SYRIZA's betrayal – along with Tsipras's unpopular 2018 agreement to recognise Greece's neighbour as North Macedonia – led to its defeat in 7 July 2019 elections. Centre-right Néa Dimokratía (ND), under chief Kyriakos Mitsotakis, formed the first Greek non-coalition government since 2009, with a commanding majority.

Mitsotakis repeated this feat after two successive elections in May/June 2023, with a strong parliamentary majority allowing him to remain in office until 2027, solidifying his position as a prominent figure in Greek politics.

IMPORTANT DATES

c. 3000 BC Foundation of Athens on and around Acropolis.

594–93 BC Solon curtails aristocratic power.

508 BC Kleisthenes introduces limited democracy in Athens.

490 BC First Persian War: Greeks win at Marathon.

480 BC Athenian fleet defeats Persians in the Strait of Salamis.

478 BC Athens unites allies under the Delian League.

449–429 BC The Golden Age of Perikles.

431–404 BC Peloponnesian War; Sparta defeats Athens.

338–323 BC Macedonians, including Alexander the Great, rule Greece.

323–146 BC The Hellenistic Period.

146 BC–AD 330 Roman rule.

AD 49–50 St Paul brings Christianity to Athens.

529 Byzantine emperor Justinian closes the pagan Athens Academy.

1204–1458 Latin Crusaders establish duchy of Athens.

1458 Athens falls to the Ottoman Turks.

1687 Venetians besiege Athens; Parthenon blown up.

1821–33 Greek War of Independence.

1834 Athens becomes the capital of Greece.

1914–23 Greeks from Asia Minor flood into Athens.

1941–44 Three Axis powers occupy Greece; the Germans hold Athens.

1946–9 Greek Civil War; Communist rebels defeated.

1952 Greece becomes a member of NATO.

1967–74 Military junta rules Greece.

1981 Greece joins the EC.

2004 Athens hosts Olympic Games for second time.

2010–13 Greek debt burden becomes unmanageable, resulting in two bailouts and crushing austerity measures.

2015 Alexis Tsipras (SYRIZA) elected prime minister as head of a coalition.

2015–16 Refugee numbers increase sharply thanks to unrest in Syria and Africa. Greece negotiates third bailout deal.

2019 Kyriakos Mitsotakis (ND) becomes prime minister.

2023 Mitsotakis re-elected; Tsipras resigns as head of SYRIZA.

Looking out over Athens and the
Acropolis from Lykavittós Hill

OUT AND ABOUT

Viewed from the air – or from the heights of the Acropolis or Mount Lykavittós – Athens forms a sprawling maze of apartment blocks and office buildings stretching to the horizon. Yet downtown Athens is remarkably compact. Ancient remains and worthwhile museums are scattered across the central area, mostly within walking distance of one another, while the metró and bus systems provide inexpensive, fairly reliable transport for those who become footsore.

Until the 1920s, Athens grew incrementally over time, resulting in numerous districts, each with its own character. This guide divides the city into a number of sections, covering the ancient centre first and then moving out in a clockwise spiral through the other important neighbourhoods.

Ancient Athens was focused on the Acropolis, with sacred temples built atop the rock and the town spread out below. Today the area is still replete with Greek and Roman remains, albeit interspersed with later buildings – a fascinating mixture of Neoclassical mansions and terraced cottages dating back to Ottoman times. This area, Pláka, is one of the most charming parts of Athens.

THE ACROPOLIS

It's impossible to overestimate the importance of the **Acropolis** ❶ (daily Apr–Oct 8am–7.30pm except Mon opens 11am, Nov–Mar until 5 or even 3pm) to the ancient Greeks. The religious significance of this sheer-sided rock, looming 90m (300ft) above Athens, was paramount, and the buildings on the summit still embody the essence of classical Greek architecture. You can see these temples from most parts of the city – particularly at night when they are

Exploring the Acropolis

beautifully lit – which adds to the feeling that this small area is still the heart of Athens. The name 'Acropolis' derives from the Greek words *ákro*, meaning 'highest point', and *pólis*, meaning city.

Try to visit early or late in the day to avoid the tour groups, or on Mondays, when most tours don't operate; wear comfortable rubber-soled shoes as there are slippery stones worn smooth over the centuries and numerous uneven areas where heels can catch. Stretches of concrete path, added in 2022 to enhance access for those with mobility issues, have proven controversial.

Once past the ticket office, a path leads to the summit of the Acropolis – a relatively flat plateau around 320m by 130m (1,050ft by 427ft) in area. This steep incline is the last section of the original route taken by the Panathenaic procession up to the statue of Athena (see page 50).

Used for strategic purposes throughout the Mycenaean and Archaic periods, the rock was easy to defend. It had spring water and uninterrupted views of the surrounding area. The first religious structures appeared at the end of the 6th century BC, though these early temples were destroyed by the Persians under Xerxes in 480 BC. The Athenians left the gutted temples untouched for three decades and were only persuaded by Perikles to undertake a reconstruction programme in 449 BC.

Perikles commissioned the Parthenon, the Erechtheion, the Temple of Athena Nike and the Propylaea, taking advantage of a new marble quarry on Mount Pendéli (Pentele to the ancients); the marble thus became known as Pentelic. When the Romans took control of Athens they embellished the site with small additions, but the decline of Roman power left the Acropolis vulnerable to attack and vandalism. The rock reverted to its earliest use as a strategic stronghold during Ottoman rule. Large quantities of stone from the temples were used for construction of bastions and domestic buildings.

Following Greek independence in the 19th century, a zealous restoration project saw the removal of all medieval and Ottoman structures on the Acropolis, and inaugurated archaeological studies of the ancient remains. These continue to the present day.

THE PROPYLAEA AND AROUND

As you make your way up towards the Propylaea (gateway) you will pass through the **Beulé Gate Ⓐ**, built as part of a 3rd-century AD defensive wall. This gate, named in honour of French archaeologist Charles Ernest Beulé was revealed only in 1853, underneath an Ottoman bastion. Immediately past this stands the jewel box-like **Temple of Athena Nike Ⓑ**, among the earliest Periclean projects, with four Ionic columns at the front and rear; since the millennium it has been completely reconstructed, using original masonry chunks. In myth, King Aegeus leapt to his death from here upon spying the ship of his son Theseus, who had neglected to change his sails from black to white as a sign of having successfully vanquished the Cretan Minotaur.

More like a temple than a gateway, the monumental **Propylaea** ❸ was a sign of things to come, built to impress visitors. It retains this ability in modern times, even though the structure was never actually completed. Construction commenced in 437 BC to a plan by the brilliant Athenian architect Mnesikles. A series of six Doric columns marks the transition into the Propylaea, beyond which there are four symmetrical rooms, two on either side of the walkway. Two

A GREEK WHO'S WHO

As the cradle of democracy, history, philosophy, drama and comedy, it's not surprising that Athens was the birthplace of some of the most illustrious figures in ancient history:

Sokrates (Socrates; *c.* 469–399 BC): philosopher and orator who pursued truth through dialectic discourse.

Plato (*c.* 428–347 BC): student of Socrates, political and religious philosopher; founded his own academy of higher study.

Aristotle (384–322 BC): philosopher; student at Plato's academy and tutor to Alexander the Great.

Herodotos (Herodotus; 484–425 BC): 'Father of history'; wrote thorough accounts of the early Persian wars and dynastic struggles in Asia Minor.

Thukydides (Thucydides; *c.* 460–400 BC): chronicled the Peloponnesian Wars with the first analytical methodology for recording history.

Perikles (Pericles; *c.* 495–429 BC): Athenian statesman during the city's Golden Age; responsible for construction of the Parthenon.

Kallikrates and **Iktinos**: architects of the Parthenon (447–432 BC).

Pheidias (*c.* 490–430 BC) and **Praxiteles** (active mid-4th century BC): sculptors.

Aiskhylos (Aeschylus; 525–456 BC), **Sophokles** (497–406 BC) and **Euripides** (480–406 BC): great tragic dramatists.

Aristophanes (448–385 BC): originator of Greek comedy.

The Propylaea seen from below

rows of three Ionic columns (this was the first building to incorporate both styles of column) support the roof, whose coffered ceiling was originally painted as a heavenly scene. The five heavy wooden doors along the walkway would have heightened the anticipation of ancient pilgrims, as each would be opened in turn. The only room to have been completed was the second on the northern side. This was used as a refuge for visitors to the Acropolis and also, according to the 2nd-century AD travelling geographer Pausanias, as a picture gallery (*Pinakotheke*), since its walls were covered with panels and frescoes.

Just beyond the Propylaea, you will find on your right remains of the **Sanctuary of Artemis Brauronia D**, founded in the 4th century BC.

THE PARTHENON

The **Parthenon E** is one of the most recognisable buildings in the world. The series of columns supporting pediment and frieze is the epitome of Athens to many visitors and would also have been to travellers

Optical illusion

There are no straight lines anywhere in the Parthenon; the ancient designers deliberately used a technique known as *entasis*, with gradual curves in lintels, stairways or pediments, and columns with bulging centres. This sophisticated optical illusion leaves the impression that the building is completely squared on the vertical and horizontal.

in ancient times. However, they would have seen a highly coloured structure decorated with magnificently carved sculptures, not to mention a strong wooden roof. What remains is the bare Pentelic marble used in the construction of the skeleton, and the refined lines and form that make it an architectural masterpiece.

The Parthenon was dedicated to Athena, goddess of wisdom and justice, and means Temple of the Virgin. It also housed the city's treasury, thus combining spiritual and secular wealth. An Archaic temple on the site was removed after the battle of Marathon in 490 BC to make room for a much larger temple. This so-called older Parthenon was still being constructed when the Persians destroyed all of the Acropolis temples in 480 BC. Work on the present temple, designed by Kallikrates and Iktinos, began in 447 BC. The temple was dedicated to Athena in 438 BC, at the Greater Panathenaic Festival. This festival then took place every four years until the late 3rd century AD (see page 50).

The Parthenon was converted into a church in the 6th century, and a bell tower was added by the Byzantines who named it Agía Sofía, meaning the Holy Wisdom. During the 15th century, under Ottoman rule, the bell tower became a minaret, and the church was converted into a mosque.

Eventually the building served as a munitions store. On 26 September 1687, when Venetian forces were besieging Athens, a shell hit the Parthenon, igniting the powder inside. The resulting explosion destroyed the centre of the temple along with many priceless carved friezes and columns. Under a 'licence' obtained from the sultan, Lord Elgin removed as much of the Parthenon's sculpture as his men could cut free, a process that continued from 1801 until 1811. These items, known as the **Elgin Marbles**, are on display in the British Museum, though the legitimacy of retaining them is hotly disputed, particularly by contemporary Greeks who refer to them as the Parthenon Marbles and unequivocally deem Elgin a vandal. Restoration on what remains of the temple has been almost constant since 1834.

THE ERECHTHEION AND PORCH OF THE CARYATIDS

To the north of the Parthenon stand the graceful statues of the **Porch of the Caryatids**, which adorn the southern facade of the **Erechtheion** ❻. This temple is an unusual mélange of styles, with rooms at vary-

ing levels, built on the putative site of Athena and Poseidon's contest for the honour of protecting Athens. It was the last of Perikles' great buildings to be finished, dedicated in 406 BC, and combined the worship of Athena and Poseidon under one roof. Following the contest between the two gods, legend has it that they were reconciled, and this dual temple recognised their special bond with the city. The sanctuary was converted into a church in the 6th century AD and was used to house the local governor's harem during Ottoman times.

The ruins of the Parthenon at the summit of the Acropolis

The **caryatids** – female figures used as pillars – are so named because they were long presumed to be depictions of the women from Peloponnesian Karyai, captured after that city-state made an alliance with the Persians and was sacked in punishment. Now, however, it is thought more likely that they represent local novices in the service of the goddess Athena. The on-site sculptures are copies: five of the originals are displayed in the New Acropolis Museum; the sixth, taken by Elgin, is in the British Museum. On the eastern facade a row of Ionic columns marks the entrance to the sanctuary of Athena Polias, established here after the original Temple of Athena was destroyed by the Persians. The foundations of this **Old Temple of Athena** are in a roped-off area directly south of the Erechtheion.

The Erechtheion's north facade consists of another porch, on high foundations since the ground level drops here. A hole in the ceiling and a gap in the floor were left to show where Poseidon had struck with his trident. The name Erechtheion derives from Erechtheos, legendary Archaic king of Athens and predecessor of Kekrops; the latter's tomb was supposedly just west of the building.

The Porch of the Caryatids

VIEWS FROM THE ACROPOLIS

When you've finished exploring the Acropolis, take time to enjoy the views from its walls, some of which date back to the Mycenaean era. From the northeast corner, by the flag-pole, you can see several of the other major archaeological sites and the district of Pláka below. The wooded slopes of Mount Lykavittós, with the smart area of Kolonáki on its lower slopes, is to the northeast. The coast and the islands of the Saronic Gulf lie to the southwest.

AROUND THE ACROPOLIS

A number of other archaeological remains – including the Odeion of Herodes Atticus, the Theatre of Dionysos, the Monument of Philopappos, the Hill of the Pnyx and the Hill of Areopagos – can be found on the flanks of the Acropolis and on nearby hills. Head south of the rock by turning left out of the main entrance and you will reach the first after a five-minute walk.

THE ODEION OF HERODES ATTICUS (IRÓDIO)

The **Odeion of Herodes Atticus** Ⓖ (the Iródio in modern Greek) was built in AD 161–174 in Roman style with a three-storey stage and an auditorium capable of seating five thousand spectators. It was destroyed during the 3rd century AD, while in the 18th century the Ottomans used material from the ruins to build a defensive wall. In the 1950s it was restored and now provides the venue for spectacular outdoor summer performances held during the **Athens and Epidauros Festival** (see page 83). Except for events, it is not open to the public.

THE THEATRE OF DIONYSOS

Set into the hillside on the southeastern flank of the Acropolis are the extensive remains of the **Theatre of Dionysos** Ⓗ (daily May–Oct 8am–7.30pm, Nov–Apr until 5pm), built in the 6th century BC and upgraded two centuries later. In Roman times, the Stoa of Eumenes, of which little remains, linked it with the Odeion of

Herodes Atticus. The theatre, capacity seventeen thousand, was the birthplace of dramatic and comic art and formed the social and political heart of Athens during its 'golden age'. The premieres of several major pieces by Sophokles, Euripides and Aristophanes were performed here, and the Athenian assembly also met here late in its history. Most interesting are the carved front-row thrones for VIPs, including one with lion's-claw feet reserved for the high priest of Dionysos; only traces remain of the Dionysos Eleutherios temple beside the theatre. The so-called **Stage of Phaedros** depicting scenes from the life of Dionysos dates from the 4th century BC.

ACROPOLIS MUSEUM

Opposite the Dionysos theatre stands the shining modern construction of the **Acropolis Museum** ❷ (Apr–Oct Mon 9am–4.30pm,

The Odeion of Herodes Atticus

Tue–Sun 9am–7.30pm, Fri until 9.30pm, Nov–Mar Mon–Thu 9am–4.30pm, Fri until 9/30pm, Sat–Sun until 7.30pm; www.theacropolismuseum.gr), inaugurated after many delays in 2009 at a cost of €130 million.

The stark, angular structure seems distinctly retrograde from outside, but the interior with its clever natural lighting does an admirable job of showcasing the contents, many never before exhibited owing to the space limitations of the old museum up on the Acropolis.

The lowest gallery houses finds from the Acropolis slopes. Leading to the upper levels is a ramp, simulating the approach to the Acropolis, surveyed by the scarred but still impressive, original Caryatids (which have recently undergone three-and-a-half years of laser cleaning). On the first floor, the Archaic exhibition features the famous Moskhophoros (Calf-Bearer), and various coquettish *korai* revealing a pre-Classical ideal of beauty in their make-up, earrings and crinkled, close-fitting garments. The top floor is the pièce de résistance: a glass gallery holding a reconstruction of the **Parthenon pediments**, of the same size and compass orientation as the actual Parthenon looming just outside the wrap-around windows. The friezes, including the triangular western aetoma, are mounted at eye level – unlike their original position overshadowed by eaves so that the ancient Athenians couldn't really appreciate them. Authentic fragments which Greece retains – less than half the total – have been mounted alongside plaster casts of the originals in the British Museum (and elsewhere), a pointed exercise in advocacy for their return.

During construction (2004–07), parts of ancient Athens were discovered on site. This was one reason for the delayed opening: building plans were altered so that dwellings, wells, water and sewage works, an olive press and even a symposium hall with mosaic flooring remained viewable through glass panels set in the ground. The excavations extend far under the museum, the latter suspended above them by one hundred massive anti-seismic columns.

PHILOPAPPOS MONUMENT

Southwest of the Acropolis stands the **Monument of Philopappos** ❸, built in AD 116 for the last titular ruler of Commagene. This small Hellenic kingdom located in southeastern Anatolia was independent from 162 BC until AD 72. When Philopappos lived in Athens as a Roman consul there was no longer a Commagene to rule but he was generous to his adopted city, which responded with this impressive funeral monument. The convex facade has a sculptured frieze depicting Philopappos riding a chariot and performing his duties in the senate. The view of the Acropolis from atop Filopáppos hill, as it is now called, is incomparable; the easiest way up is by paved path from the brilliantly frescoed Byzantine church of **Ágios Dimítrios Lombardiáris** ❹ of the 15th century, a popular venue for weddings and baptisms.

THE PNYX AND AREOPAGOS HILLS

North of Ágios Dimítrios Lombardiáris rises the **Hill of the Pnyx** ❺, meeting place of the Assembly of Athens. Loosely translated, pnyx means 'crowded or tightly packed place', and in ancient times this was a highly populated area. You'll see the outlines of walls, including the defensive **Themistoklean Wall**, among nearby shrubbery. The Pnyx meeting place can be found below the summit on the northeastern side of the hill. When democracy was established at the end of the 6th century BC, the debating chamber moved from the Agora to this structure, where prominent public figures made their speeches at the rostrum. Seats were provided for the five thousand citizens of the city needed for a decision-making quorum, who would listen to the arguments of the likes of Perikles and Themistokles. On the **Hill of the Nymphs**, north of the Pnyx, looms the Neoclassical Athens Observatory, Theophil Hansen's first project, opened in 1842.

On the north flank of the Acropolis is the **Areopagos Hill** ❻, diagonally down to the north of the main Acropolis ticket office.

PLÁKA AND ANAFIÓTIKA

After exploring these fascinating sites, you should make your way towards the modern city via two small districts offering a range of cafés and tavernas, along with images of domestic life not found in more modern parts of Athens.

Anafiótika ❼ hugs the high ground immediately below the Acropolis, and can be reached semi-directly from the Areopagos. Built during the 19th century by skilled construction workers from the small Cycladic island of Anáfi, today the narrow lanes with their neat, whitewashed cottages – less than fifty remain – and potted geraniums are still evocative of their Aegean roots.

Pláka ❽ lies below Anafiótika and fills the space between the ancient and modern city, extending almost to Mitropóleos and Filellínon streets. This was the centre of population from Byzantine times through to Greek independence. The maze of narrow, occasionally pedestrianised thoroughfares with many Neoclassical mansions and humbler houses is a delight to explore.

Pláka is particularly atmospheric in the evenings when visitors stroll before dinner and shopkeepers tout their wares on the narrower lanes; these open out onto quiet squares often dominated by Byzantine churches or older monuments. The Neoclassical buildings are now strictly protected, and this is the one

The Monument of Philopappos

The Athens Observatory, on the Hill of the Pnyx

part of the city which, superficially at least, gives a taste of what Athens was like before 1900.

PLÁKA MUSEUMS

At Níkis 39, the **Jewish Museum of Greece** ❾ (Mon–Fri 9am–2.30pm, Sun–10am–2pm; www.jewishmuseum.gr) tells the story of the various Jewish communities across the country, including the tragic events of 1943–4, when most Greek Jewry was wiped out.

At the southern end of Adrianoú, near a lovely square occupied by Byzantine Agía Ekateríni church, stands the **Monument to Lysikratos** ❿. Dating from the 4th century BC, its series of curved panels and columns create a circular structure supporting a dome made from a single block of Pentelic marble. Originally, this was topped by a bronze tripod – a prize awarded in choral competitions during the Classical era. During the 18th century a Capuchin monastery occupied the land all around the monument and the interior of the base was used as a guest room. Lord Byron stayed in 1810, supposedly penning part of *Childe Harold* here.

High up near the Acropolis, the private **Kanellopoulos Museum** ⑪ (Wed–Mon 9am–4pm; www.camu.gr) occupies a Neoclassical mansion at Theorías 12. This eclectic family collection, some housed in a stylish new wing, encompasses Geometric-to-Hellenistic-period artwork, Roman funerary ornaments from Fayum, and Byzantine icons, jewellery, frescoes and tapestries. A few doors down at Pánou 22 is an engaging annexe of the Greek Folk Art Museum, **Man and Tools** (Wed–Mon 8.30am–3.15pm; www.melt.gr), full of pre-industrial processes and implements.

CATHEDRALS OLD AND NEW

From the Kanellopoulos and Man and Tools museums, walk straight down Mnisikléous to the vicinity of Athens' two cathedrals. Ground was broken for the rather gaudy new **Mitrópolis** ⑫ in 1842; it was completed in 1862, financed by the sale of land and structures pertaining to 72 other churches.

In the shadow of the main cathedral huddles the tiny **Mikrí Mitrópolis** ⑬ (Little Cathedral), doubly dedicated to the Panagía Gorgoepikoös (She Who is Quick to Hear) and Ágios Elefthérios, a completely spurious saint whose relics are in fact the bones of a Greek Macedonian fighter from the early 20th century. Dating from the 12th century, the church was built using stone from various ancient structures. Wander around its exterior walls to see sections of Greek and Roman columns, or fragments of ornate carvings.

THE ROMAN FORUM

Where Adrianoú intersects Eólou, turn south on the latter to reach the **Roman Forum** ⑭ (daily Apr–Oct 8am–7.45pm, winter 5pm closure), first established during the 2nd century BC to accommodate an expanding Athens.

The ornate entrance gate was erected by the Athenians under the archon Nikias (11–9 BC), in honour of Athena in her avatar of Archegetis (Commander of the City). Much of the north and west wall of the Agora lies unexcavated under the houses of Pláka, but the south wall and the remains of the south colonnade are there, along with a series of shops. The most remarkable building in the complex (though it stood outside the Agora when built) is the **Tower of the Winds**. This octagonal structure was a *klepsydra* or water-clock built by a Syrian Greek, Andronikos Kyrristos, during the 1st century BC.

Just west of the Tower of the Winds you'll see one of only two mosques still standing in Athens, the **Fethiye Mosque**. Built shortly after the Ottoman conquest, it was meticulously restored during 2014–17 and is now open to the public.

THE GREEK AGORA

From the south side of the Roman Forum, continue west along Polygnótou to the southeast entrance of the ancient **Greek Agora** ⓯ (daily Apr–Oct 8am–7.30pm, closes earlier in winter), birthplace of western democracy and the social, commercial and administrative heart of the ancient city-state of Athens (*agora* is derived from the Greek *agiero*, meaning to assemble). From the 6th century BC onwards, this area played host to a number of activities including religious and political meetings, law courts, education, shopping or simply passing the time. Here Sokrates (Socrates) presented his philosophical theories; unfortunately, he fell foul of the authorities and was put to death in 403 BC.

From the southeastern entrance, follow a section of the Panathenaic Way past the 11th-century church of **Ágii Apóstoli**, the only remaining Byzantine building on the site. Greatly changed over the centuries, it was restored to its original form in the late 1950s. The frescoes in the narthex are original; others were moved from the Hephaisteion when it was deconsecrated from its role as Ágios Geórgios church. The Panathenaic Way continues to the other entrance off Adrianoú, near which lies the **Altar of the Twelve Gods**. This small monument, from where distances to all other points in the Greek world were measured, is now mostly hidden beneath a metro line. A significant section of the altar was exposed in February 2011 during maintenance work and the altar briefly became the focus of protests (and a lawsuit) by archaeologists and local *dodekathístes* (Olympian god worshippers), who objected to the metro administration's plans to re-site its tracks atop the altar rather than prepare a diversion. However, a court ruled against them, and the altar mostly disappeared again in August 2011. Directly south, within the archaeological site, outlines of the **Altar of Ares** and **Temple of Ares** can be seen in gravel. Beyond them are the remains of the huge **Odeion of Agrippa**, a roofed theatre built in 15 BC. Before it are three gigantic statues of a god and two tritons.

Museum of Paul and Alexandra Kanellopoulos, Attica

The Stoa of Attalos

The eastern side of the Agora is dominated by the **Stoa of Attalos** ⓰.
First erected by King Attalos II of Pergamon and opened in 138 BC, it
was faithfully recreated during the 1950s, giving a stunning vision of
what communal buildings were like in ancient times. Stoas were very
popular in antiquity and all large settlements had at least one. These
long colonnaded porches provided shade in summer and shelter in
winter and were often used to link important community buildings.
The Stoa of Attalos was a two-storey structure with small shops at the
back. Today it houses the excavation offices and the excellent **Stoa
of Attalos Museum** (same hours and ticket as for site). Here you'll

OTTOMAN ATHENS

Until recently locals have not been keen to highlight monuments
erected by the Ottoman conquerors, but it was the juxtaposition of
these elements of an oriental bazaar with remains of the more distant past that most intrigued the first Grand Tourists who showed
up in Athens late in the 18th century. The Ottomans did not consider
Athens an especially important town, endowing it with just three
purpose-built mosques (not counting churches converted for Islamic
worship). These were the Fethiye and Tzidarakis mosques, and the
Küçuk Tzami, just south of the Roman agora, though only foundations
of the latter remain. There were also several *hammams* (bath-houses), though the only survivor is the intriguing **Abdi Efendi baths
(Loutrá ton Aéridon)** at Kyrrístou 8 (Wed–Mon 8am–3.15pm; www.
melt.gr), built in phases from the 15th to the 17th centuries, with
exhibits illuminating both the social and hydraulic functions of the
baths nearby, opposite the Tower of the Winds, stands the surviving
gateway of a 1721-vintage *medresse* or Koranic academy, later used
as a prison and demolished around 1900.

find a wide range of artefacts from the ancient Agora site, including six bronze ballots used in the deliberations of the *parabyston* or Court of the Eleven, concerned with criminal justice. Look out too for the *ostraka*, or clay tablets, bearing the names of those banished, or 'ostracised', from Athens for ten years – Hippokrates, Themistokles and Aristeides the Just being a few of the more famous exiles.

Mikrí Mitrópolis

The Hephaisteion

The northwestern side of the Agora is dominated by one of the world's best-preserved ancient Greek temples, the **Hephaisteion** ⑰ (Temple of Hephaistos; also known, incorrectly, as the Theseion). The design of the temple, completed between 449 and 444 BC, is Doric mixed with Ionic elements. Hephaistos was the god of metallurgy, and this temple was set at the heart of the smithing, casting and ironmongery district. Later it was converted into the church of Ágios Geórgios with the addition of interior walls and a vaulted roof, surviving through Ottoman times – the last services were performed in 1834. It then served as a museum and storehouse.

The Tholos and Bouleuterion

Following the path through the Agora you'll see the round **Tholos** or **Prytaneion**, built in 465 BC as the assembly and dining hall for the *prytanes*, a governing committee responsible for the city's daily business. The fifty members of each tribal contingent took turns serving for approximately one month on this executive committee, and during this month they were fed at public expense in the Tholos. At night at least seventeen members slept here so that decisions could be made instantly in cases of emergency. Immediately north of the Tholos is the site of the original **Bouleuterion** (Council Chamber), constructed after the reforms of Kleisthenes in 508 BC; most traces of it were erased when the currently visible **Metroön** (Temple of the Mother of the Gods) was erected here during the 2nd century BC, at the time when the **New Bouleuterion** was built just to the west.

MONASTIRÁKI AND PSYRRÍ

The area immediately northeast of the ancient Greek Agora is known as Monastiráki, one of the most colourful parts of Athens.

The reconstructed Stoa of Attalos in the ancient Greek Agora

South of Ermoú, which approximately bisects the district, mostly pedestrianised streets are full of pavement cafés, shops near the cathedrals selling religious articles, more overtly touristic boutiques selling ceramics, sandals and copper kitsch, and (centred on Platía Avyssinías) the used-furniture-and-metalware **flea market**, liveliest on Sundays. North of Ermoú lie more practical, workaday shops, especially in the district of **Psyrrí ⑱**, where they co-exist with tavernas, *mezedopolía* and cafés which get fully going after dark. Ermoú itself forges east to Sýndagma Square (see page 59), with high-end retail outlets along the stretch to either side of a little square that's home to the beautiful 11th-century Byzantine church of **Kapnikaréa ⑲**. Its frescoes (interior open during daylight hours) were painted during the 1950s by Asia-Minor-born, Neo-Byzantine artist Photis Kontoglou (1895–1965). Kapnikaréa was earmarked for demolition in the 1830s but was saved by the personal intervention of Ludwig of Bavaria, father of Greece's first king.

MONASTIRÁKI SQUARE

The district revolves around **Monastiráki Square** (Platía Monastirakioú), always crowded with commuters hurrying to the Art Nouveau metro station, barrow-vendors of fruit and nuts, and buskers. The 11th-century church at its centre – **Panagía Pandánassa,** – was rebuilt in 1678 as the heart of a much larger, now-vanished convent. The south side of the square is dominated by the currently shut **Tzisdarákis Mosque ⑳**, completed in 1759 by the Ottoman governor of that name. This once contained the **Kyriazopoulos Traditional Pottery Collection** rather garish work from Asia Minor which will probably move to the new Museum of Modern Greek Culture; the building's more subtly decorated interior may prove more interesting if it re-opens.

Just up Áreos from the mosque stands **Hadrian's Library ㉑**, built in AD 132 around a garden-courtyard with an ornamental pool. Only the west wall and a stretch of colonnade are now standing, but after years of desultory excavations the grounds are now open to the public (daily Apr–Oct 8am–7.45pm, closes earlier winter).

The new Museum of Modern Greek Folklore 12, contained in various old houses embraced by the narrow streets Vrysakíou and Kládou, creeps towards completion (at the time of writing the museum was expected to open at some point in 2024).

Currently under construction, occupying the entire block of old houses formed by Áreos, Adrianoú, Vrysakíou and Kládou, the new **Museum of Modern Greek Culture** ㉒ (www.melt.gr) should become the latest addition to the Monastiráki landscape. The new museum will provide a more generous home to the long-closed Folk Art Museum on Kydathinéon, whose collection included embroidery,

THE PANATHENAIC FESTIVAL

The Greater Panathenaea was made popular by Peisistratos (ruled 561–556 and 546–527 BC). It was held every four years in summer (experts disagree during which month), to honour the goddess, Athena; a 'Lesser' Panathenaea took place annually. The festivities comprised athletic contests and musical events, and the winners were given vials containing olive oil from the fruit of the sacred groves of Athens. However, the most important element of the celebration was a procession that led from Kerameikos through the Agora along the Panathenaic Way (aka Sacred Way), finishing at the Parthenon, Athena's temple. At the head of the procession, on a wheeled ship propelled by priests, was a new embroidered garment to adorn the cult statue of Athena. This had been woven by the female guardians of the temple – the *Arrhephoroi*. Once within the sacred precincts, animal sacrifices were made before the statue was robed and the procession dispersed, but presumably festivities of some sort continued across the city for days afterwards.

lace and liturgical garments, as well as a wonderful array of paintings by the early 20th-century folk artist Theophilos Hatzimihail. Spinning and weaving should also be represented, along with traditional puppets, festival masks and costumes. Their gift shop is already functioning nearby at Adrianoú 43–45 (open summer noon to 8pm).

The 5th-century BC Hephaisteion

Another annexe, the **Museum of Greek Folk Musical Instruments** ㉓, will continue to function in its long-running premises in an 1830s mansion at Diogénous 1–3 (Wed–Mon 8.30am–3.30pm; free). This traces the history and distribution of effectively everything that has ever been played in Greece, with percussion and wind instruments on the ground floor, assorted stringed instruments upstairs and a basement full of carnival and liturgical noisemakers. Headphones allow visitors to sample the sounds made, and a well-stocked shop with literature and CDs (plus occasional concerts in the garden) complete the experience.

BENAKI MUSEUM OF ISLAMIC ART

When the Benaki Museum (see page 62) was renovated in 2000 to focus on Greek history, all the fine Islamic art objects from the collection were moved to this excellent annexe, the **Museum of Islamic Art** ㉔ (Thu–Sun 10am–6pm; www.benaki.gr), in Psyrrí district, at Agíon Asomáton 22 corner Dipýlou. Here, two converted Neoclassical mansions display over eight thousand items across four floors. They are presented roughly chronologically, and a map in each room shows the extent of polities with Islamic rulers at that time. There are astronomical instruments, decorated rifles and daggers, illuminated manuscripts, dazzling ceramics, and many other breathtakingly beautiful objects. The ornate reception room from a Cairo mansion, re-created on the third floor, is a highlight.

KERAMEIKOS, GÁZI AND METAXOURGÍO

Reaching the archaeological site of **Kerameikos** ㉕ (daily Apr–Oct 8am–7.30pm, Mon opens 11am; Nov–Mar daily 8.30am–3pm) on foot has been made far more pleasant since the western end of Ermoú – beyond Thisío metro station – was pedestrianised. It is also literally a few steps from the Museum of Islamic Art. The archaeological site incorporates a section of the 478 BC city wall, and the Dipylos gate into Athens coming from Eleusis and Pireás.

The Panathenaic Procession (see page 50) would start from the separate, **Sacred Gate** here on its journey to the Acropolis, and the procession of the Eleusian Mysteries would leave the city via the same gate along the **Sacred Way (Iera Odos)**. The most important building found here, dating in its present version from Roman times, is the **Pompeion**, where procession paraphernalia was stored and where those involved would ready themselves.

Kerameikos was named after the potters who worked here within the city walls (Inner Kerameikos), on the site of good clay deposits along the banks of the River Eridanos (still flowing, now called Iridanós). Their work was transported around the Greek world, but the pots were not considered to be of any great value, designed to be used – and broken – within a year or so.

Outside the wall (Outer Kerameikos) was the major cemetery of the city (it was forbidden to bury the dead within the city walls), with burials dating from the 12th century BC. Major figures from Greek history were interred here, and their funerary monuments are some of the most exquisite items found during excavations around the city. The site **museum** (same hours and ticket as site) exhibits burial finds dating from the 12th to 6th centuries BC.

For those whose artistic tastes lean more towards post-industrial landscapes, just beyond Kerameikos – across busy Pireós – is the old gas works of **Gázi** ㉖, with its round tank, stacks and warehouses: these have been converted into the **Technópolis** www.athens-technopolis.gr, which hosts cultural events and exhibitions. Further down Pireós at no. 138, inside a converted ex-Lada dealership, is the city's premier temporary exhibit venue: the multi-level **Benaki Museum Pireós Annexe** ㉗ (Thu & Sun 10am–6pm, Fri & Sat 10am–10pm) featuring the best in contemporary painting, photography and installations, as well as an excellent bistro. Recent top-notch exhibitions have included retrospectives of 20th-century Greek photographers Voula Papaïoannou and Kostas Balafas, Belgian artist James Ensor, and Czech photographer Josef Koudelka.

Going northeast along busy Pireós towards the centre, in the up-and-coming Metaxourgío district at Myllérou 32, corner Avdí, is the **Athens Municipal Gallery** ㉘ (daily 9am–1pm, also Mon–Fri 5–8.30pm; free), yet another of the many excellent art exhibition spaces which have opened in the city since the turn of the millennium.

Monastiraki flea market

Kerameikos funerary monument

OMÓNIA AND ENVIRONS

From Monastiráki, the parallel thoroughfares of Athinás and pedestrianised Eólou (more comfortable for walking) lead straight north to **Omónia Square** (Platía Omonías; Omónia means Concord), the apex of the traditional commercial triangle. Either street leads through the central market area, one of the most fascinating (and non-touristy) districts of Athens, where you can buy anything from live chipmunks to cinnamon sticks. Quieter Eólou offers, next to a little square with a flower market, the church of **Agía Iríni**, where superb chanting by Lykourgos Angelopoulos' choir takes place during Sunday morning services (from 9am).

Busier Athinás forges up to Evripídou with its spice stalls and the **Varvákios Agorá** ㉙, the 1870s-built meat-and-fish market on the right; the meat section works long hours, and also hosts one or two surviving restaurants serving *patsás* (tripe soup), the traditional Greek hangover cure. Fruit and vegetables are sold on Platía Varvakíou to the left, and further on, at the edge of Psyrrí, lies Athens' **'Little Asia'**, full of Bangladeshi, Pakistani and Chinese shops. **Omónia Square**, when you finally reach it, has benefitted from a 2019 redesign which included the replacement of a fountain removed in 1992, much landscaping and token traffic-calming measures.

THE NATIONAL ARCHAEOLOGICAL MUSEUM

A ten-minute walk north of Omónia along Patisíon brings you to the **National Archaeological Museum** ❸⓪ (Apr–Oct Wed–Mon 8am–8pm, Tue1–8pm; Nov–Mar Wed–Mon 8.30am–3.30pm, Tue 1–8pm; www.namuseum.gr), one of the world's most prestigious archaeological collections.

Directly ahead of you as you enter, the prehistoric collection (rooms 3–6) contains the treasure trove unearthed at Mycenae, including the exquisite gold **Mask of Agamemnon**. German-born archaeologist Heinrich Schliemann found the mask placed over the face of a body that he pronounced that of the legendary 13th-century BC King Agamemnon, but in fact it dates from more than three hundred years earlier. In spite of this, the name remains. The prehistoric rooms also have Athens' finest collection of Cycladic figures from the 3rd millennium BC. These simple, rounded female forms were funerary or devotional objects and make a stark contrast to the intricate pediment and frieze carvings and religious statuary from temples on the Acropolis. There is a rare male figure among the collection, and the beautiful **Harp Player** – a more complex carving in the same style.

Rooms 7–35 concentrate on sculpture – perhaps the greatest collection of ancient sculpture in the world – displayed to show the chronological development of the art form. Simple, idealised male and female figures (*kouroi* and *korai*) of the Archaic Age (mid-7th–5th century BC) give way to more ornate and literal human forms as you walk through the collection into the Classical Age and then on to the Hellenistic period followed by the Ptolemaic and Roman eras. Greek gods are well represented, as are various eminent human figures of Roman times, such as a bronze statue of the Roman emperor Augustus.

Room fifteen is dominated by a fine bronze statue of Poseidon (460 BC), found in the sea off northerly Cape Artemísion on the island of Évvia. The god is set to launch his trident against foes

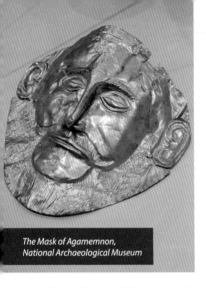

The Mask of Agamemnon,
National Archaeological Museum

unknown. The Hall of the Stairs hosts another bronze statue dredged from the sea nearby, the Hellenistic **Little Jockey**. The diminutive jockey rides a handsome steed which has its two front legs raised into the air, as if about to leap over a not-shown obstacle.

Rooms 36 to 39 contain an extraordinary collection of bronzes, including votive offerings found at the Idaean Cave in Crete – mythical nursery of the god Zeus. Rooms forty and 41 display artefacts from Egypt, especially from the Ptolemaic period when Ptolemy (a general under Alexander the Great, and therefore of Greek stock) took control of Egypt. One of his descendants was Queen Cleopatra. But perhaps the most compelling bronze in the museum's holdings is the **Ephebe of Antikythera** (c 340–330 BC), recovered near that islet by sponge divers in 1900, still retaining inlaid eyes.

FROM OMÓNIA TO SÝNDAGMA

Three major thoroughfares – Stadíou, Panepistimíou and Akadimías – run parallel between the Omónia area and Sýndagma Square. The first two boulevards have upmarket shops selling jewellery and designer labels, plus the giant Attica department store, and two modern stoas between them packed with more boutiques. These stoas were specifically mandated by the original Bavarian town plan of the 1830s and, aside from the surviving main-street grid, are its only aspect to have been faithfully adhered to.

At Paparigopoúlou 5–7 on the Sýndagma side of Platía Klávthmonos you'll find the **Museum of the City of Athens ③①** (Mon, Wed–Fri 9am–4pm, Sat–Sun 10am–3pm), housed in King Otho's first residence when he arrived in Greece in 1832, with a model of Athens as it was a decade later. Nearer to Sýndagma, on Platía Kolokotróni, is the **National Historical Museum ③②** (Sept–June Tue–Fri 9am–4pm, Sat & Sun 10am–4pm; July–Aug Tue–Sun 10am–4pm, last entry 3.30pm; free; www.nhmuseum.gr), lodged in what was Greece's original parliament building. Its permanent collection focuses mostly on the 1820s Greek War of Independence and the personalities involved, most of them shaggy mountain bandits recruited to the patriotic cause; an equestrian statue of one of them, Theodoros Kolokotronis, prances out front, pointing indignantly (says the local joke) at the building which formerly housed the Communist Party HQ. There are also worthwhile temporary exhibitions to check out.

NEOCLASSICAL TRILOGY

Panepistimíou (University Street) is officially named Eleftheríou Venizélou after the Cretan-born statesman (though no one, except for a few official cartographers, calls it that). The location here

A NEW LOOK

Following two overhauls since 2000, the National Archaeological Museum is set to undergo an even more comprehensive refit, supervised by Berlin-based David Chipperfield Architects, featuring a rammed-earth extension of 20,000 square metres, and a rooftop park. Visitors should expect full or partial closure of the existing Neoclassical galleries.

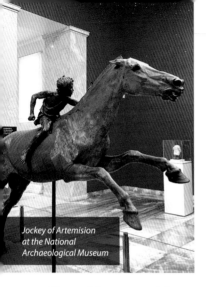

Jockey of Artemision at the National Archaeological Museum

of the original **National Library**, the **University** and the **National Academy** ㉝ confirm it as the intellectual heart of modern Athens. All three Neoclassical buildings give some idea of how the Agora of the ancient city may have looked in its prime.

The **Academy**, on which construction work began in 1859, is the most impressive of the three. It was designed by Theophil Hansen, a pre-eminent architect of his generation. The seated figures of Plato and Socrates guard the entrance and an intricately carved pediment depicts the birth of Athena; all were sculpted by Leonidas Drosos. A native of Denmark, Hansen was also responsible for the **National Library** (as well as the Royal Observatory in Athens and a number of buildings in Vienna). Hansen's brother Hans Christian designed the **University** in 1842; its portico, an attempted re-creation of the Parthenon's Propylaea, features frescoes of a seated King Otto flanked by the ancient Greek pantheon.

Continuing towards Sýndagma you will pass, at no. 12, the Ilíou Mélathron, once the home of Heinrich Schliemann and his wife Sophie. Today it houses the **Numismatic Museum** ㉞ (Apr–Oct Wed, Fri–Mon 8.30am–3.30pm, Thu 9am–7pm; Nov–Mar Wed–Mon 8.30am–3.30pm; last entry 20 min before closing; www.nummus.gr), containing an extraordinary collection of over five hundred thousand coins from antiquity to modern times. The justly popular garden café often hosts events on summer evenings, especially at full moons.

Beyond the northeasternmost thoroughfare of Akadimías lies **Exárhia**, the traditional locus of bookstores and book publishing, as well as being the student quarter, with multicoloured graffiti and posters promoting every contrarian cause – plus periodic clashes between demonstrators and police, most lately about the excavation and ruination of its central triangular platía for a new metro station

SÝNDAGMA SQUARE AND AROUND

Platía Syndágmatos ❸❺ (Constitution Square) is dominated on the east by the imposing facade of the **Parliament Building** (Voulí), originally built as the royal palace and completed in 1842. The western facade, facing the square, has a Doric portico made of Pentelic marble. In front of the building on the retaining wall is the Memorial of the Unknown Soldier, commemorating all Greeks who have fallen in war. Decorated with a modern carved relief of a Classical theme, the marble is inscribed with an oration by Perikles honouring the Peloponnesian War dead. *Évzones* – traditionally dressed, specially recruited, extra tall soldiers – guard the tomb and the presidential residence on Iródou Attikoú. The formal 'changing of the guard' takes place every Sunday at 10.45am; however,

Subdued hues

The brothers Theophil and Hans Christian Hansen designed the Academy, National Library, and University as faithful reproductions of Classical architecture in all but one respect: colour. Flecks of paint on particularly well-preserved ancient artefacts tell us that neon-garish blues, reds, oranges and yellows were the rule for ancient statuary and relief work.

the *évzones* have a changeover daily on the hour, when two new guards take the place of the previous shift – something not to not miss on your trip to Athens.

The **Grande Bretagne Hotel** ❸ on the northeast corner of the square was also built in 1842 as a sumptuous private residence and has become an Athenian institution. During World War II it served as the military headquarters of both the Germans and the British. Winston Churchill survived a thwarted bomb-plot here during his stay in December 1944. Thoroughly renovated before the 2004 Olympics, it is worth stopping in for a drink at its posh Alexander Bar (dress accordingly!).

AROUND SÝNDAGMA

Just behind the Parliament building are the verdant landscaped grounds of the **National Gardens** ❼ (sunrise–sunset; free), conceived by King Otto's queen, Amalia, who sent the new Greek navy across the globe to collect specimens. Just south of this oasis with its artificial streams and duck ponds stands the **Záppeio** ❽, an imposing Neoclassical building designed by Theophil Hansen as a national exhibition centre in 1878, set in its own gardens (24h). It now houses a modern conference centre, with a popular (if pricey) café adjacent.

A five-minute stroll from Sýndagma along Amalías (or through the National Gardens) to the junction with Vassilísis Ólgas brings you to **Hadrian's Arch** ❾, built by the Athenians for the emperor Hadrian in AD 131–32. The west side of the arch facing the Acropolis and the two ancient agoras bear an inscription reading, 'This is Athens, the former city of Theseus'. The inscription on the other side reads 'This is the city of Hadrian and not of Theseus'.

Immediately southeast looms the **Temple of Olympian Zeus** ❿ (Stíles Olymbíou Dioú; daily 8am–3pm), the largest temple ever built on Greek soil. Work began on this colossal temple in the 6th century BC but was only completed 650 years later. Hadrian dedicated the temple to the ruler of the ancient pantheon, Zeus Olympios, during the Panathenaic Festival in AD 131–32. It was imperative that the temple should be fitting for his position, and its dimensions – 96m (315ft) long and 40m (130ft) wide, with columns more than 17m (53ft) high – are truly majestic. Originally 104 columns surrounded an inner sanctum that protected a gold-and-

The Neoclassical National Library

ivory statue of Zeus which has since been lost. Today only sixteen columns are still standing, but their Corinthian capitals have a wonderful elegance.

Nearby, where Vassilísis Ólgas meets Vassiléos Konstandínou, is the **Kallimármaro Stadium ㊶**, (Mar–Oct 8am–7pm, Nov–Feb daily 8am–5pm) sitting in the lee of Ardittós Hill, and first constructed in 330–329 BC for the ancient Panathenaic Games. It was rebuilt by the city's great benefactor, Herodes Atticus, in AD 140. A modern Greek benefactor, George Averoff, sponsored the stadium's reconstruction for the first modern Olympic Games, held here in 1896. However, its length is too short and the turns too tight for modern athletic events, so the 2004 Olympic Games were held primarily at OAKA, a purpose-built Olympic complex in the northern suburb of Maroúsi. But Kalimármaro remains a popular concert and rally venue, while joggers throng the pine-covered slopes around.

VASSILÍSIS SOFÍAS AND PANGRÁTI MUSEUMS

Vassilísis Sofías, the main thoroughfare leading east from Sýndagma, passes several major embassies – and several important museums, three of them walkable from the Evangelismós metro station.

Closest to Sýndagma is the **Theoharakis Foundation for Fine Arts and Music** ⓰ (daily 10am–6pm, Oct–May Thu until 8pm, closed 1–25 Aug; www.thf.gr) at no. 9, corner Mérlin, with a changing programme of often blockbuster exhibitions and small chamber concerts. Next up is the main premises of the **Benaki Museum** ⓱ (Koumbári 1; Mon, Wed, Fri and Sat 10am–6pm, Thu until midnight, Sun 10am–4pm; free Thu; www.benaki.org), a collection donated to the state in 1954 by the wealthy cotton merchant Emmanouil Benakis, who was born into the Greek community of Alexandria. It

Sýndagma Square and the Parliament Building

is the only museum that covers all ages of Greek culture and history, and there are Greek works of art from prehistoric to modern times. There is also an excellent gift shop, frequent special exhibitions and a popular if pricy rooftop café.

Three blocks further east from the Benáki stands the **Museum of Cycladic Art** ⓮ (Neofýtou Douká 4; Mon, Wed, Fri–Sat 10am–5pm, Thu 10am–8pm, Sun 11am–5pm; www.cycladic.gr). Permanent exhibits highlight the exquisite marble figurines discovered in the Cyclades islands (c.3000–2000 BC). Most of these are female, suggesting the worship of fertility or an earth-mother religion. The museum has long been renowned for completely unrelated but excellent temporary exhibits – anything from El Greco and his school to Picasso and ancient art.

Further down Vassilísis Sofías at no. 22 is the 2004-extended **Byzantine and Christian Museum** ⓯ (Apr–Oct Wed–Mon 8am–8pm, Tue 1–8pm; winter closes 4pm; www.byzantinemuseum.gr). One of the original buildings here is a splendid 19th-century mansion built for the flamboyantly eccentric Philhellene Duchesse de Plaisance (1785–1854), who was married to one of Napoleon's associates but came to Greece, fell in love with the country, and stayed. Her mansion is no longer used for exhibits; the bulk of the artefacts, from the early Christian period right through to 13th-century Attica, are found in a huge and impressive modern underground wing. Despite being subterranean the galleries are light and spacious, and the items (including the 7th-century Hoard of Mytilene) well-displayed and informatively labelled. This stylish transformation made what was once a small and specialist collection into one of the major Athens museums.

Next door is the **War Museum** ⓰ (daily Apr–Oct 8am–7pm, Nov–Mar 9am–5pm), opened just after the 1967–74 dictatorship. Outside stand various 20th-century artillery and aeroplanes, while the interior offers a surprisingly absorbing collection of uniforms, weaponry and documents (scantily labelled in English), particularly good on Greece's tribulations during World War II – though omitting the still-controversial civil war.

Opposite Evangelismós metro station and the Hilton Hotel is the **National Gallery** ㊼, which emerged in 2022 from a ten-year complete reconstruction from the basement up (Thu–Mon 10am–5pm; Wed 12–8pm; www.nationalgallery.gr). The core collection of Greek art from just before independence to recent years does a good job of placing it in social context and as part of international trends. Few of the artists are household names overseas, but that's no reflection on their merit. Most numerous are battle scenes from the 1820s Greek uprising, but there are also religiously imbued works by Panagiotis and Nikolaos Doxaras, preceding sensitive portraits by 19th-century artists Ioannis Altamouras and Georgios Avlihos, plus the slightly later Panos Arvadinos and Periklis Cirigotis. Surrealist Nikos Engonopoulos gets a look-in, while there is also a smattering of foreign artists, including Fernando Botero. Ample display space is devoted to the abstract painter Nikos Hadjikyriakos-Ghikas (1906–1994) and the mythically inspired Alekos Fasianos (1935–2022).

Budget time and energy for the nearby, privately endowed **Goulandris Museum of Contemporary Art** ㊽ (Wed–Thu & Sat–Mon 10am–6pm, Fri 10am–8pm;

Lykavitós

Northeast of Sýndagma rises the steep, pine-covered hill of Lykavittós, which unlike Filopáppos and Ardittós was not settled in ancient times owing to a lack of water supply. Both can be reached either by an arduous walk up from the posh Kolonáki residential district, or by funicular from the corner of Aristíppou and Ploutárhou (9am–1.30am daily; €9 roundtrip including restaurant discounts).

The National Gardens

www.goulandris.gr/en/visit/be-athens), occupying an imaginatively adapted Neoclassical mansion (plus modern extension) in Pangráti at Eratosthénous 13, next to Ágios Spyrídon church. The collection includes works by Cezanne, Chagall, Giacometti, Kandinsky, Klee, Miró, Modigliani and Renoir.

EXCURSIONS

Athens is undeniably a fascinating city, but given the traffic and congestion, even the listed attractions may pall after some days. Luckily you are well placed for day or even overnight excursions, on an organised tour or under your own steam.

MONASTERY OF KESSARIANÍ

Nestled in a vale on the slopes of Mount Ymittós 5km (3 miles) east of the city centre, the **Monastery of Kessarianí** ㊾ (Wed–Mon 9am–3.30pm) and its surrounding gardens are a favourite retreat of city-dwellers. The River Ilissós rises here, nourishing the vegetation which has been a constant since ancient times; gently graded hiking trails loop through the gardens and further into the wilderness of Pendéli. The monastery compound itself encloses a refectory, Byzantine baths and the original 11th-century church, decorated with vivid frescoes of scenes from the life of Christ, painted in 1682.

At the summit of Lykavittós Hill

MONASTERY OF DAFNÍ

The ancient Sacred Way or Iera Odos (see page 50) – now traced more or less exactly by the modern Ierá Odós boulevard – heads west from Kerameikos to the edge of the city, in Haïdári district. Here in a wooded pass, 10km (6 miles) from the centre, sits the **Monastery of Dafní** (50) (Wed–Mon 9am–3pm; free), built on the site of an earlier temple of Apollo.

The monastery seen today dates from about 1080; from 1207 until 1458, when Athens was ruled by Frankish lords, Cistercian monks lived here. Reoccupation of the monastery by Orthodox monks resumed only during the early 16th century, but they were expelled during the 1820s for harbouring independence fighters. Restoration took place twice after World War II, and yet again, ongoing since 1999, when a major earthquake caused severe damage in Athens. The pretty Byzantine church is renowned for its beautiful, late 11th-century mosaics, particularly that of *Christ Pantokrator* in the main dome.

ANCIENT ELEUSIS

Continuing along the Sacred Way, which in ancient times was lined with shrines and tombs, brings you to an industrial landscape of shipyards, steel foundries and oil refineries on the Saronic Gulf – amid which, incongruously, is one of antiquity's most hallowed sites: **Eleusis** (51) (Wed–Mon 8.30am–4pm), marooned beside decidedly unromantic modern Elefsína, which was derided by poet-lyricist Nikos Gatsos' Persephone's Nightmare, set to music by Manos Hadjidakis

Eleusis was home to the Sanctuary of Demeter and the Eleusian Mysteries – a series of complex and enigmatic rituals performed by priests before an audience of male, non-slave citizens. The Mysteries thrived from the Mycenaean to the Christian eras, but the exact nature of the rites was never divulged, since all initiates kept – on pain of death – the secrets of the cult. Eleusis has suffered badly over the centuries, and the excellent site museum with finds and models of the sanctuary helps make sense of what today is largely an expanse of jumbled masonry. Modern Elefsína served as European Co-Capital of Culture during 2023, which resulted in a revamped museum and tavernas lining the pedestrianised streets around the ruins and down on the shore esplanade, plus event venues in converted ex-industrial premises.

BRAURON (VRAVRÓNA)

Some 4km (2.5 miles) east of the airport, but reached along a roundabout road via Markópoulo, lies the evocative sanctuary of **Brauron** ❷ (Vravróna; Wed–Mon 8.30am–4pm), sacred to Artemis and one of the earliest such shrines, supposedly established here by Agamemnon's daughter Iphigeneia. Another legend holds that, in atonement for slaying one of Artemis' sacred bears, the nobility of Attica were required to dedicate their young daughters as novices ('little bears') of the goddess; the 2010-revamped site **museum**, 1.5km (1 mile) further (same hours), is full of small-girl figurines holding various live offerings to the goddess, or dressed in bear-masks. The green site itself, watered by a still-flowing sacred spring, features the 5th-century BC **Stoa of the Little Bears**.

SOÚNIO (SOUNION)

The peninsula of southern Attica extends into the Aegean Sea, and at Soúnio – its most windswept tip – the ancient Greeks built a beautiful **Temple of Poseidon** ㊸ (summer daily 9am–sunset, from 9.30am in winter), god of the sea, earthquakes and horses. The views from here are beautiful whatever the time of day – but the sunsets are particularly spectacular. The temple itself is one of the finest in Greece. Of the original 34 Doric columns only sixteen are still in situ, and the ornate frieze on the pediment and entablature has been ravaged by the salty air, but the whole effect of the building combined with the setting – a sandy beach on one side and a sheer drop on the other – is magnificent. The site is also home to many guinea fowl.

Sounion is reached by following the coast road from the capital 70km (43 miles) southeast through several resort-suburbs with both fee-payable and free beaches.

PIRAEUS

Just 10km (6 miles) southwest of Athens, and almost indistinguishable from the sprawling capital, is **Piraeus** ㊵ (Piréas), actually the fourth-largest city in Greece, and the country's largest container port. Although most people just use Piraeus as a departure point for the islands, there are a few attractions. Coming from central Athens, lines 1 or 3 on the metro brings you to within walking distance of the numerous distinct quays or *aktés* accommodating swarms of ferries, catamarans and hydrofoils. The best coastal promenade away from the qiaus leads south from the cruise-ship terminal on Aktí Xavierou south to Akti Thmistokléous, lined with little coves, places to eat and spectacular views.

THE SARONIC GULF ISLANDS

The Saronic Gulf islands – Égina (Aegina), Póros, Ýdra (Hydra) and Spétses – are closest to Athens. Hydrofoils or catamarans for these islands depart from Aktí Miaoúli at Piraeus, slower conventional ferries just opposite from Aktí Posidónos. Note that there are very few connections between Égina and the other islands.

At busy times like Sunday evening, all sea-craft back towards Piraeus sell out, so buy a return ticket or see to it immediately upon arrival.

Monastery of Kessarianí

Égina (Aegina)

On the closest island to the mainland, just 45 minutes distant by hydrofoil, the pretty quayside of **Égina (Aegina) town**, with its Neoclassical buildings, awaits as you disembark near the whitewashed chapel of Ágios Nikólaos, protecting the harbour entrance. Walk along the water's edge past the colourful fishing fleet, have lunch at a taverna in the marketplace or buy some of the pistachio nuts for which the island is renowned. Égina is a delight out of season but can be very busy on warm weekends; many wealthy Athenian families have second homes here. The resort of **Agía Marína** is 15km (9 miles) from the town on the east coast and has a good, child-friendly beach. Just before, stop off at the 5th-century BC Doric-order **Temple of Aphaia** (Apr–Oct daily 8am–8pm, Nov–Mar daily 10.30am–5.30pm), set on a hilltop amidst pines, equalling Soúnio in appeal.

Póros

The volcanic double-island of Póros lies less than 150m (465ft) from the Greek mainland, off the northeastern coast of the Argolid Peninsula and an hour from Piraeus by hydrofoil or catamaran. Small sailing boats throng the narrow straits, a summertime yachtsman's paradise. **Póros town** – the only settlement on the smaller island – is a maze of narrow winding streets rising up a small hill with a clock tower. The seafront is the hub of all activity, with tavernas and cafés lining the waterside. The rest of Póros, called Kalávria, is covered with verdant pine forest, while the coastline is dotted with small pebbly coves – great for swimming or sunbathing, but crowded.

The only other sights, both on Kalávria, are the **Monastery of Zoödóhou Pigís**, above the island's best beach, and the foundations of a **Poseidon temple** are well inland near the top of the island. Here the famous Greek orator Demosthenes chose suicide in 322 BC rather than surrender to Macedonian forces. It was originally excavated by the Swedish School of Archaeology at the start of the 20th century, and new digs by the same organisation are underway.

Ýdra (Hydra)

Just over an hour and a half from Athens by hydrofoil or catamaran, Ýdra (Hydra) is the most celebrated of the Saronic Gulf islands, and the approach into its harbour the most dramatic. The beautiful port of **Ýdra Town** remains hidden until the very last moment, and when the panorama comes into view your camera should be ready. Above the narrow cove the hillsides are blanketed with Neoclassical mansions. There are no cars in Ýdra town except for the odd rubbish truck and mechanical digger, only donkeys which transport almost everything up the slopes. There are few beaches, where the water is generally clear, and there is some excellent walking.

During the 1950s and 1960s the island was a film location (*Boy on a Dolphin*, *Phaedra*, *Girl in Black*) and artist colony, prior to becoming an upscale resort and cruise-boat stop. Pricey jewellery boutiques intermingle with craft galleries, exclusive restaurants, surprisingly inexpensive tavernas and chic cafés.

Spétses

At well over two hours away from Piraeus, **Spétses** is the remotest of the Saronic Gulf islands and just a bit too far to do as a day-trip. The town, while not as immediately striking as Ýdra's, has a similar architecture and straggles pleasantly along the north coast for several kilometres. Unlike Ýdra, motorised vehicles are not totally banned on Spétses, though private cars are prohibited in the town itself – horse-drawn buggies, scooters and a few conventional taxis are the main alternatives. Away from town, Spétses has the best beaches and cleanest water of any Saronic Gulf island, easily explored by hired boat or scooter.

THE ARGOLID PENINSULA

The history of ancient Greece is punctuated with the feats of city-states led by great leaders, of which Athens is, of course, the most famous. Within a day's journey of the capital lies the **Argolid Peninsula**, a region of the Peloponnese where the sites of two such city-states – Corinth and Mycenae – can be viewed. Those with more time should definitely visit the ancient Theatre of Epidauros and the port city of Návplio.

View over Póros

The Corinth Canal

An engineering marvel, the **Corinth Canal** cuts the

narrow isthmus that links the Peloponnese with the Greek mainland and divides the Saronic and Corinth gulfs. Sailing around the Peloponnese took considerable time and exposed ships to some of the most dangerous waters in the Mediterranean – especially in winter. Ancient Greeks ported huge vessels across the 6km (4-mile) wide isthmus, and as early as AD 67, the Roman Emperor Nero was making the first attempts at cutting a canal. It would not become a reality until 1893 when, after 11 years of digging, a channel was opened for shipping. Its modest dimensions, however, made it obsolete almost immediately, even more so in the contemporary era of supertankers. Today it is used mostly by yachts – and bungy-jumpers, who launch themselves from the pedestrian catwalk below the road bridge (June–Aug Tue–Sun 10am–5.45pm, May, late Sept and Oct Sat–Sun only) courtesy of Zulu Bungy (www.zulubungy.com), closed some days in winter.

Bronze gods

A somewhat long walk from the Dimoikó Théatro metro staion , at Hariláou Trikoúpi 31, the Archaeological Museum of Piraeus (Wed–Mon 8.30am–3.30pm), is a rather dour building hiding a wealth of artefacts found during local excavations – or dredged by chance from the seabed nearby. Pride of place goes to a 6th-century BC life-sized bronze of Apollo, displayed along with similar statues of Artemis and Athena.

Ancient Corinth

In ancient times Corinth rivalled Athens for power and influence. It mimicked the layout of the larger city – a town radiating out from the base of a rocky promontory which supported a temple of Aphrodite – though Acrocorinth is far higher and larger than the Acropolis.

Corinth was an active and prosperous city between the 8th and 5th centuries BC, founding many colonies and competing fiercely with

Athens; it sided with Sparta against Athens during the Peloponnesian Wars. During the Hellenistic period the city was economically prosperous despite political instability. After 224 BC when the Achaean League was formed, Corinth became a centre of independent Greek political life. This brought it into direct conflict with Rome, which razed Corinth to the ground in 146 BC.

Corinth Canal

The site was unoccupied for just over one hundred years, until Julius Caesar began to rebuild the city in 44 BC; revitalised, Corinth soon became the capital of the Roman province of Ahaea. The city developed its two ports (Kenhreai to the east and Lehaion to the west of the isthmus) and was flourishing when St Paul arrived on his first visit to Corinth in 50/51 CE, when he successfully established a community of believers.

During the 3rd and 4th centuries Corinth suffered attacks by the Goths and a major earthquake in 375. The 6th century saw another earthquake and Slavic raids, after which the city was abandoned.

The modern, uninteresting city of Corinth lies several kilometres northeast of **ancient Corinth** (mid–Apr–Aug 8am–8pm, Sept until 7/7.30pm, Oct until 6/6.30pm by date, Nov 8am–5pm; Dec–Mar Wed–Mon 8.30am–3.30pm). Most prominent as you approach the site is the Doric **Temple of Apollo**, built in the 6th century BC and one of the oldest buildings in Corinth. Many other remains date from the Roman era, including ornate facades of the **Fountain** of Peirene, where you can still hear the waters flowing through cavities at the rear, and the Lehaion Way, with cart tracks clearly visible worn into the marble slabs.

The Bema (platform), traditionally believed to be where St Paul stood before the Roman consul, is situated to the south side of the agora. The site museum (same hours and ticket) contains many interesting finds and features a number of dioramas depicting Corinth as it would once have looked.

After visiting the ancient city, head uphill to take in the magnificent site of Acrocorinth (daily 8.30am–4pm). Fortified since the 7th century BC, the summit is still encircled by high masonry walls continually reinforced during the Byzantine, Frankish, Venetian and Ottoman eras. At the summit, within three layers of protective walls, are the remains of a Temple of Aphrodite, an early Christian Basilica, Byzantine cisterns, a Frankish tower, the upper Peirene spring plus Ottoman mosques and hammams.

Nemea

Some 19km (12 miles) further down the motorway from ancient Corinth, ancient Nemea (mid-Apr–Aug daily 8am–8pm, Sept closes 7/7.30pm, Oct closes 6/6.30pm; winter opening uncertain) is well worth the short detour west. A sanctuary rather than a town, its highlight is a massive Doric Temple of Nemean Zeus; nine of its columns, and two architraves, have been re-erected by UC Berkeley excavator, Stephen Miller. A good site museum and stadium 1km (0.6 miles) north, with the oldest entrance tunnel known, round out the attractions.

Mycenae

From the 15th to the 11th century BC, this rocky outcrop was one of the most important centres in the known world, seat of the mighty Mycenaean empire which grew to encompass mainland

The Lion's Gate, erected during the 13th century BC

Greece and most Aegean islands. The exploits of the Mycenaeans, and their greatest leader Agamemnon, were thought to be myth until – in the 1870s – the archaeologist Heinrich Schliemann set out to find evidence of Homer's stories in (until then) strictly legendary Troy and Mycenae. He successfully uncovered both sites, and thereby transformed the world of archaeology – and man's view of history.

Schliemann found the remains of the city of **Mycenae** (Mykínes; daily Apr–Aug 8am–8pm, Sept until 7/7.30pm, Oct until 6/6.30pm, Nov–Feb 8.30am–3.30pm, Mar until 4pm) buried under millennia of debris in a sheltered valley some 60km (37 miles) south of Corinth. It was so well hidden that the site had been completely forgotten, and amazingly unplundered by tomb robbers.

The military might of the Mycenaeans had been well documented by Homer, but nothing could prepare Schliemann's team for the artistic treasures unearthed here. As they dug through the remains, the tombs of several royal personalities were discovered; each skeleton lay where it had been carefully buried, its face covered in a mask of pure gold. Exquisite statuary and intricate jewellery found in the family tombs below show a softer side of these enigmatic people and bring the world of Agamemnon to life. All the artefacts from the site were taken to Athens, many now displayed in the National Archaeological Museum (see page 55).

Mycenae's massive **Cyclopean walls** – huge, rough-hewn masonry blocks laid atop one another with extreme precision, and without mortar – are so called because later Hellenes could not believe that humans were responsible for the construction and so gave the credit to the one-eyed giants of myth. The outer walls, which measured up to 14m (46ft) wide, date from around 1250 BC; they surround and protect the citadel through which the only entrance is the **Lion's Gate**, decorated with the earliest known monumental sculpture in Europe.

Just beyond the gate, look down to the right to see **Grave Circle A**, where the royal graves were found, then climb to the summit remains of the Royal Palace, from where the views of the surrounding countryside are superb. Outside the walls are three *tholos* (beehive) tombs, including the **Treasury of Atreus**, otherwise known as the **Tomb of Agamemnon**, constructed in about 1330 BC. The masonry – again eschewing the use of mortar – is superb, as is the reverberating echo irresistible to noisy school children.

Epidauros

Southeast of Mycenae, some forty minutes' drive via Návplio, is another ancient site also renowned for its acoustics. The extraordinarily well-preserved **Theatre of Epidauros** (Epídavros; daily Apr–Aug 8am–8pm, Sept until 7/7.30pm, Oct

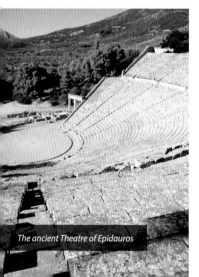
The ancient Theatre of Epidauros

until 6/6.30pm, Nov–Mar until 5pm) was built in the late 4th century BC and could accommodate an audience of twelve thousand people. It has startling acoustics: you may not hear the proverbial pin drop in the centre of the stage while you are sitting in an upper row, but you can certainly hear quiet speech. Performances are staged here every summer, as part of the **Athens and Epidauros Festival** (see page 83). The theatre was part of a much larger **Sanctuary of Asklepion**, one of the most important therapeutic centres in the ancient world, which has been extensively restored since 2010.

Návplio

The beautiful port town of **Návplio** makes the perfect base for touring the region, or perhaps a spot to have lunch while on a day-trip. Set on the south coast of the Argolid, it has been a strategic strongpoint for centuries and has no less than three interlocking castles dating from Byzantine and Venetian times on the towering rock of Palamídi, plus a fourth on the rock of Akronavplía. The city retains much of its Venetian and Ottoman past in the form of churches and mosques and served as the capital of newly independent Greece from 1829 until 1834. Here, also, Greece's first president, Ioannis Kapodistrias, was assassinated on 27 September 1831.

Formal attractions include an **archaeological museum** (Wed–Mon Apr–Oct 8.30am–4pm, Nov–Feb 8.30am–3.30pm, Mar until 4pm) in a former Venetian barracks, with finds from all the local sites, and the excellent **Peloponnesian Folklore Foundation** (Mon–Sat 9am–2.30pm, Sun 9.30am–3pm; www.pli.gr). Many tavernas set out tables in the lanes and squares of the architecturally protected old town, while the seaside promenade has locals and Athenians alike strolling in the evening. Look out towards the tiny fortified island of **Boúrtzi**; the Venetian castle there has variously been the residence of the town's executioner and a luxury hotel.

After extensive restoration and adaptation, it opened in 2023 for visits during peak season daily 9am–8pm.

DELPHI

The advice of the oracle at **Delphi** (Delfí; daily summer 8am–8pm) was available to all who were willing to make the pilgrimage to the Sanctuary of Apollo, nowadays a three-hour journey on a modern road from Athens, on the flanks of Mount Parnassós.

In ancient times Delphi was the spiritual centre of the Greek world, and no important decisions of state were made without consulting the oracle here. The cult flourished from the 8th century BC to the 4th century AD. The resident priestess (*Pythia),* a woman in her fifties who sat inside the Temple of Apollo, fell into a trance when Apollo entered her as his medium. Her unintelligible mutterings were interpreted by the temple priests, who in turn would give often ambiguous answers to supplicants.

A modern road cuts through the ancient remains, and the approach to the site from the parking area leads up a sacred way, past many treasuries and offerings dedicated by various city-states,

BASES FOR DELPHI

Modern, coach-clogged Delfí village may not appeal as a base for ancient Delphi and Ósios Loukás. Alternatives include stone-built **Aráhova**, 11km (7 miles) east on the slopes of **Mount Parnassós**. Teeming (like Delfí) in winter with skiers from nearby **ski resorts** up the mountain, it is much quieter during summer. Another possibility, 24km (16 miles) south on the shores of the Itean Gulf, is 19th-century **Galaxídi**, with Neoclassical architecture, beaches plus comfortable accommodation and tavernas aimed at Athenian weekenders year-round.

The Tholos, Delphi

to the magnificent **Temple of Apollo**, reconstructed by French archaeologists. By the roadside flows the **Kastalian Spring**, where pilgrims would purify themselves before consulting the Pythia. Just below the road and the spring are the remains of a large gymnasium used by athletes competing in the Pythian Games, and the temple of **Athena Pronaia**, where pilgrims would make their first devotional stop on the climb to the sanctuary. The most impressive building at this lower site, of uncertain function, is the circular **Tholos**, built in mottled stone. The local **museum** (Wed–Mon Apr–Oct 8am–8pm, Tue 10am–5.30pm 9am–4pm) displays an extraordinary collection of statuary and other artefacts found at the site, the most famous exhibit being the 5th-century BC bronze statue of the **Charioteer**. Other items include two enormous 6th-century BC *kouroi*, and a life-sized votive bull fashioned from hammered silver and copper.

ÓSIOS LOUKÁS MONASTERY

Located 35km (22 miles) southwest of Delphi, the **Monastery of Ósios Loukás** (daily 8.30am–3.30pm) is considered to be one of the finest Byzantine buildings in the country. Mosaics in the 11th-century church, especially in the narthex, are superb, rivalled in Greece only by those at Dafní, Néa Moní on Híos, and a few in Thessaloníki.

Athens' vibrant nightlife

THINGS TO DO

ENTERTAINMENT

Athens comes alive after dark with a range of activities; however, you'll probably need to alter your normal routine to enjoy it as locals do. Theatre or cinema performances are followed by a late, leisurely dinner, often after 11pm, and musical club performances begin at around midnight.

For most Greeks, the traditional taverna – eating, drinking and often singing with friends – is still the favoured choice for a night out. Other options include trendy bars (barákia), especially in Psyrrí, Gázi, Roúf, Keramikós and Metaxourgío districts; live venues with jazz, Greek music or rock; dance clubs with a techno, house or ambient soundtrack; and musical tavernas where food prices reflect the live entertainment. Doyenne of these, since 1999, is **Technopolis** (www.athens-technopolis.gr), with nine event venues scattered across the indoor and outdoor spaces of the former city gasworks; highlights of its calendar are a July jazz festival and a summer full-moon festival.

Other bars and clubs are scattered across the centre, and in the districts of Monastiráki Psyrrí, Thisío, Keramikós (often near the metro station) and Metaxourgío. The cutting edge of 'hipness' moves further north and west every year, but accounts of the death of Pysrrí in particular are greatly exaggerated. Evergreen venues include rooftop café-bars **A is For Athens**, at Miaoúli 2–4, and **six d.o.g.s** (Avramiótou 6–8), also an arts/performance space; boozers **Baba au Rhum**, Klitíou 6, specialising (no surprise there) in rum-based concoctions; **The Clumsies** at Praxitélous 30, for exotic cocktails; **Barrett** at Protogénous 11, with good music too; **Booze Cooperativa** at Kolokotróni 57, as much an exhibition

Theatre of Herodes Atticus

space and event venue as a bar; and adjacent **Noel** at Kolokotróni 59B, with exotic, Catholic Church-themed cocktails.

THEATRE, CINEMA AND MUSIC

The ancient Greeks were credited with inventing drama and comedy, and this tradition carries on into the present. The city has numerous active **theatres** at peak winter times, though the season lasts from October to May, and you might make a special effort to see a play in the magnificent theatre at Epidauros (see page 76). All performances are in Greek. From late May to late September, **open-air cinemas** *(ta theriná)* operate in many neighbourhoods. Screenings are typically at 9pm and 11pm (8.30pm and 10.30pm in September), and films – usually from the preceding winter – are subtitled, with the original soundtrack. The best programmed and most central are Thiseion near the Acropolis, Aigli by the Záppio, Cine Paris in Plála, Zephyros in Petrálona district, Riviera and Vox in Exárhia, Ekran in adjacent Neápoli, Oasis and Pallas in Pangráti, and Athinaia and Dexameni in Kolonáki. If you follow new art or foreign releases, check what's on at the **Tainiothíki tis Elládos** (Greek Cinematheque) at Ierá Odós 48 (www.tainiothiki.gr), which stages autumn film festivals.

From October to May a full programme of classical music and some dance and jazz plays at the **Mégaro Mousikís** (Athens

Concert Hall; tel: 210 72 82 333; www.megaron.gr). The **Lyriki Skini** or national opera company (tel: 213 08 85 700; 9am–9pm, www. nationalopera.gr) has had a new home since 2018 in the stunning, Renzo Piano-designed **Stavros Niarchos Foundation Cultural Centre** (www.snfcc.org) towards the sea at Syngroú 364, where symphonies, opera, ballet and 'musical theatre' are staged either in the main hall with its impeccable acoustics or a smaller 'alternative' venue. Free daytime guided tours are offered by the National

SUMMER FESTIVALS

The **Athens and Epidauros Festival** currently runs from June through early August and features choral concerts, dance and recitals. Since 1955 they have been staged at the open-air **Herodes Atticus** theatre below the Acropolis, with world-class performers both foreign and Greek; more recently the **Mégaron Mousikís**, a venue at **Pireós 260** and the **small amphitheatre at coastal Paleá Epídavros** have handled nearly as many events. On Fri and Sat nights during late June, July and August the **main ancient theatre of Epidauros** stages ancient Greek plays presented in modern Greek or foreign languages.

For information and tickets, go online (www.aefestival.gr or ring the ticket information number (tel: 211 8008181 (Mon–Fri 10am–6pm), from late April). Alternatively, visit the main box office at Sýndagma Square (Mon–Fri 9am–8pm, Sat 10am–6pm); the Herodes Atticus box office on the day of the performance (noon–2pm and 6–9pm); or the box office at ancient Epidauros (Mon–Thu 9am–7pm, Fri–Sat 9am–9pm).

The **Rematia Festival** at the Evripideio Theatre in the northern suburb of Halándri (www.theatrorematias.gr) occurs from early July to late September.

Library (relocated here from Panepistimíou in the centre) and the event venues.

TRADITIONAL MUSIC AND DANCE

Greece has a rich legacy of folk dance and music; however genuine, spontaneous performances are hard to find in the capital. From late May to late September the **Dóra Strátou Folk Dance Theatre** stages traditional Greek song, dance and music in its own open-air theatre below the Philopappos monument, in Petrálona (mid-July to late Sept Thu–Fri at 9.30pm, Sat–Sun 8.30pm; occasional nights late May to early July; www.grdance.org/en).

SPORTS

Athens' proximity to the coast allows you to combine **beach activities** with a city holiday. You'll find a full range of sports on offer, from tennis, windsurfing, kiteboarding and waterskiing to snorkelling and scuba. However, the nearby submarine world can be disappointing, and the water is not generally considered clean enough for bathing anywhere north of Álimos.

Much of Athens closes down during August (though not those businesses relating to tourism), when people head to the coast, the mountains or the islands. **Beaches** are busy throughout the school holidays, approximately from 11 June to 10 September. The closest resort to the centre is **Glyfáda**, only 12km (7 miles) away. About 14km (8.5 miles) distant is **Voúla**, a bit less crowded than Glyfáda, and **Kavoúri**, with a pleasant seaside promenade (including a few tavernas), just beyond. **Vouliagméni** lies just over the hill from Kavoúri, its highlight the mineral-spring-filled spa-lake at a constant temperature of 22–29°C (www.vouliagmenilake.gr); daily summer 8am–8pm, last entry 7.30pm €16–19 admission depending on the day of week, includes all amenities. There are some luxurious hotels in both Voúla and Vouliagméni, and each of these resorts has at least one beach with changing facilities, food and watersports. An entrance fee of €5–10 is typical. One of the better beach-bar-restaurant combos is *Bolivar* back in **Álimos** (www.bolivar.gr), €5–10 depending on day (includes sunbed). You'll find clean, free sandy beaches at **Anávyssos**, **Saronída** and **Soúnio**, accessible by KTEL Attikís buses rather than urban lines.

The **Saronic Gulf islands** have a longer season, from May to October, owing to foreigner patronage. Égina (Aegina) does not have the best sea; you may prefer nearby Angístri islet for swimming. Póros, Ýdra and Spétses generally have clean water, adequate beaches and offer organised watersports.

SAILING

Summer **sailing** is very popular with Athenians, as regular regattas and the crowded marinas at Piraeus, Álimos and Glyfáda all testify. Several companies hire boats with crew, or 'bare' if you have a skipper's certificate. Try, for example, Fyly Yachting and Partners at Amfithéas 10, Paleó Fáliro (tel: 210 98 58 670; www.fyly.gr); MG Yachts, Makaríou 2 corner Posidónos, Kalamáki (tel: 210 98 30 153; www.mgyachts.gr); or Sailing Athens (tel: 215 52 59 494, www.sailingahens.com) at

Swimming in the west of Ýdra

Ágios Kosmás marina, offering luxurious half- or all-day catamaran cruises, including to Cape Soúnio. Conditions for windsurfing and kite-boarding are excellent at Loútsa, on the east Attikí coast, where Nissakia Surf Club (www.nissakia.gr) caters to enthusiasts.

SCUBA

The **Attikí peninsula**'s southwest coast has many rewarding dive sites. The following outfitters come recommended for either a certification course or (for qualified divers) trips out: Athens Divers Club in Anávyssos (tel: 22910 53461, www.athensdiversclub.com) or Aqualized, also in Anávyssos (tel: 22911 59651, www.aqualized.com), or Diving Store in Lagonísi (tel: 22910 79686, www.diving store.gr).

SKIING

The closest skiing facilities can be found at **Mount Parnassós** (www.onparnassos.gr/en/parnassos-ski/parnassos-ski-center; see page 55), nearly three hours' drive from the city, where there are twenty or so mostly intermediate runs open from December to April, weather (especially high winds) permitting. The hotels and tavernas of modern Delfí and Aráhova lie twenty minutes' drive from the slopes. Aráhova is also full of outfitters for renting or buying equipment; these – and lift passes – are comparable in cost to that of the Alps or Pyrenees.

FOOTBALL (SOCCER)

Football is a national obsession in Greece, and Athens' first division (Superleague) teams (Panathinaïkós, AEK, Paniónios and Atrómitos), plus Olympiakós of Piraeus, feature prominently in domestic and European competition. The season runs from September to May, with matches on Wednesday nights and Saturday afternoons. Panathinaïkós plays at its revamped stadium on Leofóros Alexándras; AEK matches are held at their 2020-opened Agía Sofía stadium in Néa Filadélfia suburb. Olympiakós' Karaïskáki stadium is in Néo Fáliro, at the end of one tram line. Ask hotel reception for assistance in obtaining match tickets.

Shopping in Monastiráki

SHOPPING

Athens offers abundant shopping opportunities, not only for typical Greek-style souvenirs, but for haute couture, art and jewellery. Whatever your budget, you are bound to find something exciting to take home – whether a mass-produced item or a unique hand-finished piece. Individual districts specialise in certain types of goods.

WHERE TO SHOP

For undeniably tacky, mass-produced kitsch, head for **Pláka**, where such outlets are interspersed with galleries, t-shirt shops and numerous street hawkers selling novelty toys or handmade budget art. The warren of streets around the cathedral offers religious souvenirs – *thymiatíria* (incense burners), icons and *támata* (votive offerings) being the most portable.

Monastiráki is part of Athens' old bazaar area; at the Sunday **flea market** on and around Platía Avyssinías (see page 49) you can find old metalware, dishes, memorabilia and furniture, while an array of small shops on Iféstou sells everything from used

Reproductions of ancient Greek statuary

CDs and beads to army-surplus-type clothing. The covered **Varvákios market** (see page 54) between Athinás (on the west) and Eólou (to the east) offers a range of packaged Greek foodstuffs to take home.

The **Kolonáki** district is an Athenian favourite for boutiques and home-furnishing stores selling the best of European design; prices match (and sadly sometimes exceed) quality here. Ermoú, Eólou and Stadíou streets are where you will find more middle-of-the-road shops, most of them outlets of international chains, selling everything from shoes and clothing to household wares. There are also Greek department stores such as Attica, inside the Citylink complex at Panepistimíou 9 (www.atticadps.gr) and Notos Home at the Golden Hall at Kifisías 37A in Maroússi, accessible by bus or car only.

WHAT TO BUY

Copper and brassware. Copper and brass (tinned inside) have long been used for household utensils, and skilled craftsmen still work in small, central workshops. Newly made goods have a bright patina that mellows with age; some of the older pieces – including water ewers, bowls and covered pilaf vessels – are exceptionally beautiful. Ornate Ottoman-style trays (*siniá*) meant to be set on folding wooden bases will just fit in your luggage, as will serving ladles and goats' bells. The best sources of antique copperware are the stalls on Platía Avyssinías. New copperware is sold at a few shops on Iféstou.

Ceramics. Exquisite hand-thrown and painted copies of ancient pieces are available at a price, though you can also buy less expensive factory-produced items. Traditionally shaped urns, jugs and cups are decorated with scenes depicting the lives of ancient mortals or the Greek gods. Modern ceramic artists also thrive, showcased in various small galleries.

Statuary. If you want a (licit) little piece of ancient Greece, then you will have no trouble finding your own reproduction copy of a deity or a Classical statue. Plaques depicting ancient friezes or masks to hang on walls are also extremely popular, as are "Mycenaean" helmets.

If Classical statuary is too ornate for your taste, then copies of the minimalist Cycladic idols are to be found at the Museum of Cycladic Art. Similarly, both the Benaki Museum and National Archaeological Museum offer high-quality copies

DODGY DEALS

Prices are fixed everywhere but the flea market, so that's the only place you can really haggle. If you find a deal that is too good to be true for ancient coins, they're probably fakes. Bear in mind that if they're real you're not supposed to take them out of the country anyway. The same applies to all antiquities, with many court cases mounted overseas by the Greek authorities to secure the return of items illegally purchased or otherwise obtained by museums and galleries. Therefore, if you intend to buy an old piece, always use a reputable dealer and obtain an export permit, failing which you will be treated as a smuggler.

of items from their collection. Each comes with a certificate of authentication. The National or Byzantine and Christian museums also have fabulous shops stocked with postcards and high-quality books.

Folkloric items. The new folk museum complex in Monastiráki is not yet ready, but their museum shop is already working at Adrianoú 43–45 (summer daily 10am–8pm)

Leatherware. Goat- and cowhides are worked into a range of footwear, bags and clothing, though quality is generally more rustic and bohemian than similar items produced in Italy or France.

Carpets and needlepoint. The carpet-weaving tradition was largely introduced by Asia Minor refugees. Look for hand-knotted ornate patterns in wool or silk, which come with a hefty price tag.

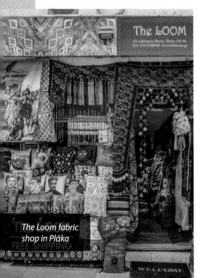

The Loom fabric shop in Pláka

The Loom at Adrianoú 94 (www.theloomcarpets.com) specialises in Greek woven goods, including blankets and embroidery. Alexandros Carpet at Patróou 8–10, corner Mitropóleos 25 (www.alexandercarpet.gr) sells a wide selection of reasonably priced rugs, both new and antique.

Needlepoint, crochet and embroidery – once activities undertaken by every Greek woman – are dying arts, so any hand-crafted pieces will become collectors' items. Machine-produced pieces are readily available as tablecloths, napkins, cushion covers and handkerchiefs.

Jewellery. Greece has been renowned since ancient times for its workmanship in gold and silver, and many high-class jewellery stores in Athens still produce superb-quality items, also utilising imported precious stones. Prices are very competitive as gold is sold by weight, with a relatively small mark-up for the craftsman's skill.

Although not strictly speaking jewellery, worry beads or *kombologiá* – carried by many older Greek men to calm their nerves – are extremely decorative. The best worry beads feature red coral, black coral, horn, bone or amber, with silver decoration and silk thread. A reputable central shop is Kombologadiko (www.kombologadiko.gr at Amerikís 9).

Icons. These are religious portraits, usually of a saint or sacred event. At the heart of Orthodox worship, they serve as a focus of prayer and a window to the divine.

For centuries, icons were popular souvenirs of a grand European tour or religious pilgrimage. However, modern production methods, using thin artificial canvas and gaudy synthetic colours, reduced their popularity. In recent years, however, there has been a rebirth of traditional icon-painting methods, both in church renovations and commercially. Natural pigments and egg tempura binding are painstakingly mixed and brushed onto a canvas bound over wood. Gold leaf is then applied, and the image is given a patina.

Pre-1821 icons will require an export permit. You will find mass-produced icons in many tourist shops, but for quality pieces, visit a specialist store or the Byzantine and Christian Museum's shop.

Engravings. There are numerous reproductions about, but for genuine antiquarian engravings at reasonable prices head for Emmanouil Drousos (daily) at Normánou 8, just off Platía Avyssinías.

Edibles and drinks. Non-perishable foodstuffs from the Greek countryside include honey, herbs, olives or olive oil, and pasta like *hilópites* or *trahanás*. For an alcoholic souvenir, try *oúzo* – the aniseed-flavoured national aperitif, *tsípouro* – similar but preferably unflavoured –or Greek brandy, which is slightly sweeter than French cognac. Metaxa is the main brand; its star rating (from three to seven) denotes strength and age. Five-star satisfies most drinkers.

CHILDREN'S ATHENS

Athens requires some forethought if you are taking young children. Not all will be eager to spend days at the ruins, and summer weather can be oppressively hot. However, children will be welcomed almost everywhere they go.

Eminently child-friendly are the National Gardens (see page 60) with their duck ponds and playground, and the 2022-revamped Pédion Áreos, near the National Archaeological Museum, also with play facilities. The Hellenic Children's Museum at Vasiléos Georgíou B 19, access from Rigíllis, near the Byzantine and Christian Museum (Fri 5–8pm, Sat–Sun 11am–3pm, closed late July–mid-Sept; www.hcm.gr/english/ free; must ring 210 33 12 995 to book a visit slot) has plenty of hands-on activities for youngsters; so too does the Herakleidon Museum at Iraklídon 16 in Thisío (daily Apr–Oct 10am–6pm; Nov–Mar Wed–Sun 10am–6pm, last entry 5.15pm) with its interactive Educational Robotics, and displays on ancient Greek technology, including the Antikythera Mechanism.

Alternatively, a boat trip to a nearby island makes a wonderful day's outing (see page 68), with numerous destinations only one or two hours distant. If all else fails, a day at the beach should blow city cobwebs away (see page 84).

WHAT'S ON

1 January: Protohroniá or St Basil's Day, a time of parties and gifts; the traditional greeting is *Kalí Hroniá*.

6 January: Epiphany (Ta Ágia Theofánia). Crucifixes are thrown into harbours on all coastlines. Young men dive for the honour of retrieving them; the winners receive good luck for the coming year.

February–March: Carnival; masked revellers take to the streets; harmless plastic hammers are sold to hit each other over the head. Meat tavernas are booked out on Tsikhnopémpti (Grill-Smell Thursday).

Clean Monday (Katharí Deftéra): First day of Lent, 48 days before Easter, marked by kite-flying and outings to the countryside.

25 March: Greek Independence Day/Festival of the Annunciation; military parades.

Early April–Early May: Easter (Páskha). The most important Orthodox holiday. Candlelit processions in each parish follow the flower-decked funeral bier of Christ on Good Friday Eve. The resurrection Mass at midnight on Holy Saturday concludes with deafening fireworks and the relaying of the sacred flame from the officiating priests to the parishioners, who carefully take the lit candles home. On Sunday, lambs are roasted signifying the end of the Lenten fast. *Note that Orthodox Easter seldom falls on the same weekend as Roman Catholic or Protestant Easter.*

1 May: May Day (Protomagiá), marked by flower-gathering excursions to the country – and massive parades by the political Left.

15 August: Dormition of the Mother of God (Kímisi tís Theotókou/Panagías). Processions and festivals across the country, starting the evening before.

28 October: Óhi Day (*óhi* meaning 'no'), commemorating Greek defiance of the Italian ultimatum of 1940. Patriotic parades.

Early or mid-November: Athens Marathon commemorates arrival of the news of the defeat of the Persians – though held in a cooler month than the battle (Aug–Sept).

December: Carols (*kálanda*) are sung door-to-door on the evenings of the twelve days of Christmas. On New Year's Eve, adults play cards for money, and a cake (the *vassilópita*) is baked and served with a coin hidden inside.

FOOD AND DRINK

The backbone of Greek cuisine is local, seasonal ingredients at their peak of flavour, served raw, or cooked simply – on a grill, flash-fried, or slow-baked. Greeks have relied for centuries on staples like olive oil, wild herbs, seafood and lamb or goat's meat, along with an abundance of fresh vegetables, fruit, grains and pulses, washed down with local wine. The traditional – and now endangered – Greek diet is one of the healthiest in the world, and prices in all but the flashiest establishments afford excellent value. The prevalence of vegetable and dairy dishes makes eating out a delight for non-meat eaters, though vegans may have a harder time.

There are numerous places to eat traditional Greek fare across Athens, but, like most other European capitals, it also offers international cuisines as well, in particular Italian and Asian. Greeks love to eat out (large parties should reserve in advance), and new restaurant openings are avidly reviewed in the local press. Both Greek and foreign-cuisine restaurants are listed at the end of this chapter (see page 104), but the following information will help you to get the most from any Greek eatery.

WHERE TO EAT

You will find a range of Greek eating establishments, each type specialising in certain dishes, and many still family-run. The *psistaría* offers charcoal-grilled meats, plus a limited selection of salads and *mezédes*. The *tavérna* is a more elaborate eatery, offering the pre-cooked, steam-tray dishes known as *magireftá*, as well as a few grills and bulk wine. Restaurants (*estiatória*) and *inomagiría* (wine-and-food canteens) overlap considerably with tavernas, though are less likely to have grilled items. The *mezedopolío* (aka *ouzerí*) purveys not just grape-pomace distillates like *oúzo or tsípouro*, but also *mezédes* dishes that complement them – spirits are never drunk on an empty stomach. Octopus, olives, a bit of cheese or a platter of small fried fish are traditional accompaniments, but lately you may choose various other hot and cold vegetable or meat dishes. For sticky cakes, retire to a *zaharoplastío* – pastry or sweet shop – or patronise one of the burgeoning number of stalls selling very good ice cream (*pagotó*) of Italian gelato calibre.

The *kafenío* is the Greek coffee shop, traditionally a men-only domain, and still so in the countryside. Usually very plainly decorated (though tables and chairs are smarter of late), it is the venue for political debate and serious backgammon (and card) games. Only drinks – both alcoholic and soft – are served as a rule.

Rooftop restaurant with a view of the Acropolis

Mealtimes

Lunch is eaten between 2.30 and 4.15pm. Traditionally this meal would be followed by a siesta before work began again at 5.30pm, but this custom is on the wane in Athens. Dinner is usually eaten from 9pm onwards, with some establishments taking last orders as late as midnight. If you want to eat early, some tavernas begin service at around 6.30pm, but most don't even open until 7pm. You will have your choice of table then, but the atmosphere is definitely better later. Sunday evening and part of or all of Monday are typical times of closure for tavernas which do not operate daily.

WHAT TO EAT

You will usually be given an extensive menu (often in both Greek and English); items currently available will have a price pencilled in beside them. However, your waiter is a more reliable guide to what is available each day; the menu is most useful for checking that the taverna is within your budget – especially for typically pricey items like meat or fish. It is also the rule to inspect the steam trays or chiller case to see what looks and smells enticing; this is a good way to familiarise yourself with the various Greek dishes.

All restaurants charge per person for a serving of usually mediocre bread which costs €0.70–1.20 per person; you have the right to refuse the bread if you say so when ordering.

Smoking

All restaurant interiors are non-smoking by law and since 2019 the government is stepping up indoor enforcement, with draconian penalties for flouting the rules. If you wish to smoke overtly, this must be done outside.

Appetisers

Carefully selected appetisers (*mezédes*) can constitute a full meal. Shared by the whole table, they are a fun and relaxing way to eat – you

Tzatzíki, crispy fried aubergine and gígandes

have as little or as much as you want. *Mezedopolía* in particular have no qualms about taking orders for '*mezédes* only' meals, bringing your choices out on a *dískos* or tray – though there is an optional second round of hot mains, often made-to-order.

The most common appetisers are *tzatzíki*, a yoghurt dip flavoured with garlic, cucumber and mint; *dolmádes*, grape or cabbage leaves stuffed with rice and vegetables – rarely mince – which can be served hot (with egg-lemon sauce) or cold (with yoghurt); *fáva*, yellow split-pea mash; *taramosaláta*, cod-roe paste blended with breadcrumbs, olive oil and lemon juice, ideally greyish and not hot pink; *skordaliá*, garlic-and-potato sauce served with fried vegetable slices; *gígandes*, large haricot beans in tomato sauce; *kalamarákia*, deep-fried small squid; *tyrokafterí*, spicy cheese dip; and *hórta*, boiled greens either wild (tastier) or cultivated. *Saganáki* is hard cheese coated in bread-crumbs and then fried, while *féta psití* is feta cheese wrapped in foil with garlic and herbs – often spicy ones – and baked.

Fresh seafood platter

Greek salad or *horiátiki saláta* (usually translated as 'village salad') consists of tomato, cucumber, onion, green peppers and olives topped with feta cheese. Cruets of olive oil and wine vinegar are found with other condiments on the table, though per a (much disregarded) January 2018 law, the olive oil is supposed to be supplied in tiny, sealed bottles and charged for.

Fish and seafood

Athens' proximity to the sea means that fresh fish (*psári*) is readily available, and throughout Attikí you will find excellent seafood restaurants (*psarotavérnes*). The day's catch is displayed on ice inside a chiller case for you to make your choice, which will be weighed, uncleaned, before cooking – check prices first as seafood is always a relatively expensive option. If the seafood is frozen or farmed (very likely from June to September), this must by law be stated on the menu – though often only in the Greek-language column, or simply with an asterisk.

Larger fish is usually grilled and smaller fish fried; all are served with fresh lemon and *ladolémono* (olive oil with lemon juice). Most common species are *barboúni* (red mullet), *koutsomoúres* (goatfish mullet), *xifías* (swordfish), *tsipoúra* (gilt-head bream) and *fangrí* (bream). *Marídes* (picarel), *gávros* (anchovy) and *atheŕína* (sand smelt) are served crisp-fried; *sardélles* (sardines) are usually grilled, then ideally butterflied. *Gónos* (hatchling) is a term applied to tiny fish or small squids. More elaborate seafood dishes include *okhtapódi krasáto*, octopus in red wine and tomato sauce; *soupióryzo* (cuttlefish with rice and spinach) or *garídes* (prawns) in a cheese sauce (*saganáki*). Fish soup, *psarósoupa*, is found only during the cooler months.

Meat and casserole dishes

Meaty take-away snacks include *gýros* (thin slices of fatty pork cut from a vertical skewer and served with tomatoes, *tzatzíki* and lettuce in pitta bread), or *souvláki* (small chunks of pork or rarely lamb cooked on a skewer). Sit-down barbecued dishes include whole chickens, sides of lamb or *kondosoúvli* (rotisseried pork), all cooked to a melting perfection. If you want a basic pork or veal cutlet, ask for *brizóla or spalobrizóla respectively*; lamb or goat chops, however, are *païdákia*. *Pansétta* is a reliable pork main, more like American spareribs than pancetta, the Italian belly bacon.

Greece's most famous slow-cooked oven dish is probably *moussakás* – successive layers of potatoes, aubergine and minced beef topped with a generous layer of béchamel sauce. It should be firm but succulent, and aromatic with nutmeg; good restaurants make a fresh batch daily.

Cheeses

Greek cheeses are made from cow's, ewe's or goat's milk, or blends of two milks in varying proportions. The best-known cheese is *féta*, popping up in every Greek salad or served alone garnished with olive oil and oregano. *Graviéra* is the most common hard cheese, varying in sharpness; there are also many sweet soft cheeses such as *myzíthra*, *manoúri* and *anthótyro*.

Dessert

Most tavernas bring a plate of seasonal fresh fruit or semolina halva as a free finale to your meal, the *kérasma*; for something more

Taverna fruit platters

Complimentary platters of fruit (*froúto*) typically feature watermelon or Persian melon in summer; grapes, kiwis or pears in autumn; sliced apples with honey and cinnamon much of the year; and citrus fruit or strawberries in early spring. Greece imports just a few temperate fruits from Italy or Spain.

substantial, the *zaharoplastío* (sticky-cake shop) dishes out some of the more enduring legacies of the Ottomans, who introduced incredibly decadent sweets: *baklavás*, layers of honey-soaked flaky pastry with walnuts; *kata-ïfi*, 'shredded wheat' filled with chopped almonds and honey; *galaktoboúreko*, custard pie; or *ravaní*, honey-soaked sponge cake. If you prefer dairy desserts, try yoghurt topped with local honey; *kréma* (custard); *ryzógalo*, cold rice pudding, obtainable at *galaktopolía* (milk shops).

WHAT TO DRINK

Anise-flavoured *oúzo* is taken as an aperitif with ice and water; a compound in the anise flavouring makes the mix turn harmlessly cloudy. The most popular brands (like Mini and Plomari) come from the island of Lésvos. *Tsípouro* is a mainland variant of this grape-mash distillate, usually without anise. Another similar distilled spirit is *tsikoudiá* which originates from western Crete, though east Cretans refer to their own as *rakí*.

There are a dozen brands of mass-market beer produced in Greece, as well as imports. Foreign brands made under licence include Amstel, Fischer, Kaiser and Heineken; local labels are Fix (reckoned the best), Eza, Mamos, Alfa, Mythos, and Vergina, also available as a strong amber ale. Any one of these will be sure to complement your culinary experience in Athens.

For a digestif, Metaxa is the most popular domestic brandy, sold (in ascending order of strength and aging) in three-, five- and seven-star grades.

Greek bottled wine has improved enormously in the last few decades; top-quality domaines include the Peloponnese (especially Nemea and around Trípoli), Macedonia (especially Drama, Amýndeo and the Halkidikí peninsula), Santoríni and Kos.

Non-alcoholic drinks

Hot coffee (*kafés*) is served *ellínikós*, 'Greek' (generic Middle Eastern) style, freshly brewed in copper pots and served in small cups. It will automatically arrive *glykós* (quite sweet) unless you order *métrios* (medium) or *skétos* (without sugar). Don't drink to the bottom as that's where the grounds settle! Instant coffee (called 'Nes' irrespective of

Enjoy a drink in Pláka

brand) has conquered Greece; more appetising is *frappés*, cold instant whipped up in a blender with sugar and milk *(gála)*, especially refreshing on a summer's day. Most cafés and bars serve Italian-style espresso and cappuccino – though expect to pay Italian-plus prices; *freddocíno*, cold cappuccino, appears in summer. For fans of milky Seattle coffee, Starbucks can be found at various Athenian locations.

Soft drinks come in all the international varieties, while juices are usually out of cardboard cartons, though fresh-squeezed-juice bars now proliferate. Bottled (*enfialoméno*) still mineral water is typically from Crete or the Greek mainland mountains. Souroti and Epsa are the most widespread domestic sparkling brands. Soda water is usually Tuborg.

BULK WINE AND RETSÍNA

Most tavernas offer house wine in bulk – ask for *krasí hýma* or *varelísio* – which is almost always cheaper than bottled varieties. It comes in full, half or quarter-litre measures, served either in coloured aluminium cups called *kantária,* or in glass flagons. This basic, rustic wine – whether red, white or rosé (which in Greece is often very dark) – will be served young and cool (cold in the case of white or rosé). Quality varies considerably; If in doubt, order a quarter litre to start with, and/or a can of soda to dilute it. Bulk wine is usually *aretsínato* (unresined), rarely *retsína* (white flavoured with pine resin). *Retsína* has been around since ancient times, when Greeks accidentally discovered the preservative properties of treating wine with pine resin. It complements the olive-oil base of oven-cooked dishes perfectly, but can be an acquired taste and should be served well chilled. The best bulk *retsína* traditionally came from Attikí's Mesógia district, but nowadays there are also good bottled brands like Malamatina, Georgiadi and Kehri.

TO HELP YOU ORDER

Could we have a table? **Boroúme na éhoume éna trapézi?**
May we order, please? **Na parangíloume, parakaló?**
A litre/a half litre (of wine) **Éna kiló/misó kilo krasí**
I'm a vegetarian/vegan **Íme hortofágos/végan**
The bill, please **To logariazmó, parakaló**

plate **piáto**	butter **voútyro**
napkin **hartopetséta**	sugar **záhari**
cutlery **maheropírouna**	salt **aláti**
glass **potíri**	pepper **pipéri**
bread **psomí**	oil **ládi**

MENU READER

fried **tiganitó**	cultivated amaranth greens **vlíta**
baked **sto foúrno**	
roasted **psitó**	summer runner (green) beans **ambelofásola**
grilled **sta kárvouna**	
stuffed **gemistá**	aubergine/eggplants **melitzánes**
fish **psári**	chickpeas **revýthia**
small shrimp **garídes**	cheese **tyrí**
octopus **okhtapódi**	wine **krasí**
small red mullet **koutsomoúres**	beer **býra**
big red mullet barboúni	(chilled) water **(pagoméno) neró**
tomatoes **domátes**	
olives **eliés**	lamb **arní**
wildgreens **hórta**	

USEFUL EXPRESSIONS

Kalí órexi Bon appétit
Kalí synnéhia Enjoy the rest of your meal (literally 'Good continuation')
Yiámas Cheers (as a toast)

WHERE TO EAT

Most of the following recommendations are central and/or close to public transport routes. Price ranges indicated are for dinner per person with modest intake of wine, beer or *tsípouro/oúzo*.

€€€€	**over 45 euros**
€€€	**35–45 euros**
€€	**22–35 euros**
€	**under 20 euros**

EXÁRHIA & NEÁPOLI

Atitamos €€ *Kapodistríou 2, metro Omónia, tel: 210 33 00 864*. This friendly, *inomagerío-mezedopolío* offers a short, somewhat meat-heavy Crete-based menu (the name means 'dittany herb') and excellent bulk wine from Límnos. *Arní lemonáto* (lemon-sauce lamb) or *thrápsalo* (deep-water squid) are good choices, preceded by a mini-salad of baby spinach leaves and *manoúri* cheese. Booking is recommended on weekends. Limited sidewalk seating: the wood-and-stone interior is inviting. Open daily (even Aug) noon–1am.

Pinaleon € *Mavromiháli 152, Neápoli, metro Ambelókipi, tel: 210 64 40 945*. This indoor-only taverna enjoys a cult following for its rich *mezédes*, mains such as smoked pork loin in *mastic* sauce or pork *kotsí* (shank), and own-brewed red wine. Usually lively, with close-packed tables, so best to book, especially Wednesdays when there's usually live music. Open late Sept–mid-May, Tue–Fri 7pm–1.30am, Sat 7pm–midnight, Sun until 10.30pm.

Rakoumel € *Emmanouíl Benáki 71, metro Omónia, tel: 210 38 00 506*. A favourite among several Cretan-cuisine spots in Athens, with delicacies like fennel pie, rosemary-sauteed snails, Sfakian sausages and seasonal greens imported from Crete; and of course, *paximádia* (rusks) instead of bread, and Cretan *rakí* by the carafe or Réthymno organic dark beer. Seating on the sidewalk or inside. Open daily lunch and dinner.

Tivoli Live €€ *Emmanouíl Benáki 34, metro Omónia, tel: 210 38 30 919.* Durable mezedopolío with live music Saturday night (booking mandatory) when high-quality rebétika musicians play. Food covers all bases from brizolákia (boneless pork chops) to kolokythoanthí gemistzei (cheese-stuffed squash blossoms). Open Mon–Fri noon–midnight, Sat noon–3am.

KOLONÁKI

Filippou €–€€ *Xenokrátous 19, metro Evangelismós, tel: 210 72 16 390.* Since 1923, this estiatório has served honest fare such as *mince-stuffed courgettes under avgolémono sauce, kolokythópita* (baked courgette pie) and *prassórizo* (leeks with rice), washed down with excellent bulk wine. Service is low-key but efficient; the dining room has a pleasantly retro air (aside from the ever-changing menu, presented on tablet devices) with proper table napery, stone flooring and MOR wall art. Small outdoor terrace, plus a few sidewalk tables opposite. Open daily lunch and dinner, except Sat eve, Sun and part of Aug.

Oikeio €€ *Ploutarhou 15, crn Alopekís, metro Evangelismós, tel: 210 72 59 216.* Meat, seafood and vegie dishes are evenly balanced at this creative cooking taverna with its quirky interior plus a few sidewalk tables. Service can be leisurely. Open Mon–Sat 12.30pm–midnight, until 1am Fri & Sat; Sun lunch in summer.

Il Postino €€ *Grivéon 3, pedestrian lane off Skoufá, metro Panepistimíou, tel: 210 36 41 414.* A genuine *osteria* with an unpretentious menu, supervised by an Italian chef with an illustrious track record in Athens. Sit in the quiet cul-de-sac outside or inside with its old-photo décor and retro music. Peroni draught beer. Open Mon–Sat 2pm–late.

KOUKÁKI/MAKRYGIÁNNI/PLÁKA

Garyfallo Kanella € *Odysséa Androútsou 35, corner Zan Moreá, metro Syngroú-Fix, tel: 210 92 45 332.* Old-fashioned, indoor-only (air-con) inomagerío with cheerful, well-lit decor: *broderie anglaise* curtains, woven chair cushions, rural impedimenta hung up, a street-scene mural. Best-value lunch in the area, where the constantly changing menu might have *angináres ala políta* (artichoke stew), *pastítsio*, or baked *pérka* fish with rice, accompanied by superb hýma wine from Límnos. Efficient, friendly service. Open Mon–Sat, noon–6pm.

Dosirak €€ *Voulís 33, metro Sýndagma, tel: 210 32 33 330,* www.dosirak-athens.gr. Mostly Korean restaurant with standards like bimbimbop, jigue, dumplings and spicy BBQ pork, but also Japanese platters like duck teriyaki, sashimi and sushi. Open daily noon–11.30pm.

Mani-Mani €€€–€€€€ *Falírou 10, metro Acropolis, tel: 210 92 18 180,* www.manimani.com.gr. Installed on the top floor of a graceful interwar house, this established nouvelle-Greek-cuisine, meat-strong restaurant does (as the name implies) still have a few specifically Peloponnesian dishes like *sýnglino* (streaky pork) risolles and quail on the menu, but it has broadened its menu to various *mezédes*, salads, pasta dishes and even token seafood, as well as creative desserts. Open daily 2–11pm.

Mikri Venetia €–€€ *Georgíou Olymbíou 15, metro Syngroú-Fix, tel: 213 02 59 158.* "Tastes and Distillates" is the motto of the oldest establishment on this popular pedestrian walkway. Tastes include grilled kebabs, Xánthi-style *kavourmás (meat stir-fry)*, Anatolian *pastourmás*-stuffed turnovers or even green curry with prawns and coconut. Seating outside or in the quirky interior. Exceptionally full drinks list, not just 'distillates'. Open daily noon–1am.

MONASTIRÁKI/PSYRRÍ

Feyrouz € *Karóri 23, corner Agáthonos, off of Eólou, metro Monastiráki, tel: 213 0318 060,* www.feyrouz.gr/en. Chef/co-owner Feyrouz, from Antakya in Turkey, dishes out an assortment of Arabic and Turkish dishes including *lahmatzoún* (Syrian/Armenian pizza), cheese- and vegetable-based turnovers, Bosphorus-style rice, intriguing soups, and several Asian puds. It's meant as 'street food' so seating is limited to just a few counter stools. Brief beer list only. Open Mon–Thu noon–10pm, Fri/Sat noon–11pm. Cash only.

Kapnikarea €€ *Hristopoúlou 2, corner Ermoú, metro Monastiráki, tel: 210 32 27 394.* The food at this *mezedopólio* – sausages, *saganáki*, aubergine dishes, good salads – is only slightly bumped up in price thanks to the acoustic *rebétika* musicians who play here every afternoon. Seating is outdoors in this pedestrianised lane, with awnings and heaters for winter. Daily lunch only, may open Thu/Fri/Sat eves too, closed summer.

Nikitas € *Agíon Anargýron 19, metro Monastiráki, tel: 210 32 52 591.* Probably the oldest (1967-founded) surviving taverna in Psyrrí, Nikítas purveys a short but sweet menu, as well as daily specials like oven-baked cheese pie, turkey burgers or wild *spátha* greens. Drink means beer, excellent *hýma* wine (try the rosé) or *óuzo*. For excellent value you can't beat it, especially if seated outdoors under the trees beside Agíon Anargýron church. Open Mon–Sat noon–8pm.

Thanasis € *Mitropóleos 69, tel: 210 32 44 705,* www.othanasis.com. Competing *souvlatzídika* (souvlaki stalls) cluster here just before Platía Monastirakioú, but queues for takeaway make it obvious which is the best. Thanasis' speciality is Egyptian-style kebab, minced beef blended with onion and a secret spice combination. The side dish of 'spicy' chilli peppers will blow your head off, beware. Open Mon–Fri 9am–2am, to 3am Sat/Sun.

OMÓNIA

Klimataria €–€€ *Platía Theátrou 2, metro Omónia, tel: 210 32 16 629.* An excellent source of hearty cooking with dishes such as pork with mushrooms or two-year-old lamb with *stamnagáthi* greens – the row of *gástres*, the traditional backcountry stew pots, tip you off as you enter. There are also vegetarian and fish choices (such as *dolmádes gialantzí*, cheese-stuffed peppers) and stuffed *thrápsalo* (deep-water squid), with barrel beer and wine. As per the name, the interior is festooned with vines. Enjoy top-notch live acoustic music on Fri–Sat from 10pm, also Wed–Thu summer and Sun after 4pm (booking mandatory). Open daily noon–1am.

Kriti (aka Takis) € *Veranzérou 5, inside the arcade, Platía Káningos, tel: 210 38 26 998.* The oldest and still among the best of Athens' Cretan tavernas, run by a family from Sitía (where the bulk wine comes from). Tuck into little platters of Sfakiá sausages, cheese- or greens-stuffed turnovers, goat-based dishes, *kolokythokeftédes* (courgette risolles) and marinated fish. Cretan music on the sound system. Success means that Kriti has expanded from a single premises to a complex of three contiguous ones. Open Mon–Sat noon–midnight.

PANGRÁTI

Baba Ghanoush € *Empedokléous 25, Platía Varnáva, tel: 212 10 50 351*, www. babaghanoush.gr. Veggie/vegan spot geared up for takeaway but with ample seating, including some outside. Besides the eponymous dish, there are fine falafels, salads (try the black beluga lentil), quinoa-sweet potato burger, houmous with pita, Syrian desserts and a limited beer/wine list – or homemade lemonade. Open Tue–Sun midday–midnight.

Colibri €€ *Empedokléous 9–13, no metro, tel: 210 70 11 011.* An established, superior pizza, burger (twelve kinds) and pasta outfit. Salads are scrumptious, thin-crust pizzas excellent value in two sizes, and red bulk wine a bargain. The owner once ran a restaurant in Sweden, and the kitchen is scrubbed top to toe nightly – so no rancid-oil smells here. Outdoor tables on the pedestrian street are much sought after in summer. Open daily 1pm–12.30am.

Karavitis €€–€€€ *Arktínou 33 and Pafsaníou 4, metro Evangelismós, tel: 210 72 15 155.* Pangráti's last surviving 1930s taverna, relying on baked casseroles, a few *mezédes* or grills, and *Mesógia* bulk wine. Traditional desserts like quince or semolina halva; outdoor seating in a lovely garden across the street, winter indoors under the wine barrels. Open daily for dinner, Fri–Sun also lunch.

Katsourbos €€ *Amýnda 2, Platía Proskópon, tel: 210 72 22167*, www.katsourbos.gr/home/. Creative Cretan cooking, with tables both inside and out. Signature dishes include *stamnagáthi* (spiny chicory)-based salads and *gamopílafo* (wedding pilaf), washed down with bulk wine, *rakí*, or organic beer from Réthymno. Open daily 1pm to midnight.

PETRÁLONA

Kappari €–€€ *Doriéon 36, metro Petrálona, tel: 210 34 50 288. Mezédes – plevrótous* under balsamic sauce, *fáva*, Anatolian pastourmadópita – in particular shine at this courtyard taverna, while mains include snails and clay-pot *moussakás*, plus some seafood. Good choice of tipple, attentive service a bonus. Open daily noon–1am, summer too.

Oikonomou €€ *Tróön 41, corner Kydantidón, metro Petrálona, tel: 210 34 67 555*. Crowded pavement tables rather than the sign over the door announce you've come to this *inomagerío* which does just a handful of homestyle dishes daily, in big portions: cabbage *dolmádes*, stewed okra, roast meat, a limited range of starters. There's hýma red wine or good *retsína*. Inside, enjoy old, coloured engravings of Attica and caricatures of wine-drinkers. Open Mon–Sat dinner only.

Santorinios € *Doriéon 8, metro Petrálona, tel: 210 34 51 629*. Cult taverna installed in an old refugee compound and barrel-making workshop from 1926; seating is in small rooms or the lovely courtyard. There's a limited menu of Santoríni starter platters, plus an array of grills (including lamb chops by weight) accompanied by decent island bulk wine – go for the red. If some dishes and frequently distracted service rate only three-and-a-half stars, the atmosphere and low prices merit four to five. Open Sept–June Tue–Sat dinner only, Sun lunch & dinner. July–Aug Sun lunch only.

BEYOND ATHENS

Albatros € *Konstandínou Sathá 36, Galaxídi, tel: 22650 42233*. Very congenial taverna run by an older couple and their daughter, whose daily-changing offerings might include rabbit stew, *gemistá*, octopus in wine, baked pies or the house speciality *samári* (pansétta in sauce). Tables indoors, or outside under trees strung with fairy lights. Open daily dinner, short lunchtime service.

Anamniseis apt'a Limania €€ *Aktí lánthi (main port quay), Galaxídi, tel: 22650 42003*. Waterside eating here can be a minefield for the unwary; this is a fair-priced spot with excellent fare, particularly seafood both simple and elaborate, good *hýma* wine and friendly service. Noon until late in season, weekends only in winter.

Geladakis (tou Steliou) € *Lane behind/east of fish market (officially Panagióti Irióti 50), Égina Town, tel: 22970 27308*. Perennial seafood classic with no airs and graces, just obviously fresh octopus, squid, swordfish and shellfish (grilled or fried) plus a bare minimum of starters or side dishes like *hórta* but a maximum of *oúzo*, *tsípouro* or bulk wine. Open daily lunch/dinner.

Ta Votsala €€ *Thymári district, 55th km Soúnio road, tel: 22910 38368*. Getting an affordable meal anywhere near the Soúnio temple and its beach is a major problem; this seafood taverna on the inland side of the Saronic-coast road 7km north makes a good solution. All usual *mezédes* – plus in spring/summer *almýra* (marsh samphire) – are present and correct, there's plenty of choice in tipple, and fishy things are patently fresh. Great sunsets. Open all day until late.

To Vyzandio €€ *Vassiléos Alexándrou 15, Náfplio, tel: 27520 21631*. Much the best, and the best value, of the old-town eateries down towards the water, but several blocks inland on a quiet pedestrian lane. Lots for vegetarians/vegans as well as grilled meat/seafood mains and the usual range of drinks including a superior beer list. Reservations suggested at night.

TRAVEL ESSENTIALS

PRACTICAL INFORMATION

A

ACCOMMODATION

Hotels. Since a pre-Olympic Games overhaul of most Athens hotels, very little remains here that could be called budget accommodation, at least of the savoury variety – count on paying at least €70 for a double room, which figure should include municipal tax and VAT. Most hotels appear on generic hotel-booking websites or have their own site.

Prices fluctuate across the year, with a difference of as much as fifty percent between high and low seasons. Savvy travellers have learned that Athens is at its most pleasant in May–June and September–October, and these are now reckoned peak seasons by most hoteliers; it can be easier to secure a vacancy during July and August, but you should book well ahead year-round to avoid disappointment. Reservations of less than three nights may attract a surcharge.

I'd like a single/double/family quad room **Tha íthela éna monóklino/díklino/tetráklino**
How much do you charge? **Póso hreónete?**

AIRPORT

The **Elefthéríos Venizélos airport** serving Athens is 27km (18 miles) from Sýndagma Square in the heart of the city. The airport **express bus** X95 (24h) will take you directly to Sýndagma Square in just over an hour if traffic is light (almost two hours in heavy traffic); departures are every 15–20min during the day, every 20–25min between 11pm and 5am. At peak traffic times, and with light luggage, consider alighting at the Ethnikí Ámyna or Nomismatokopío metro stations and continuing your journey into town from there, but this works out more expensive (if quicker) than using the infrequent (half-hourly) **metro** all the way from the airport station. If you're headed out straight to the islands, or a beach suburb, it makes most sense to use the X96 express bus, which links the airport roughly half-hourly day and night with Karaïskáki Square in Piraeus via Vári, Vouliagméni, Voúla and Glyfáda.

The fare for all express buses is €5.50 at press time and the ticket is only valid for a single journey into town, without using the metro. Buy your ticket at the kiosk outside the arrivals hall and validate it on the machine as you board the bus. The metro ticket costs €10 for a single traveller, €18 for two persons, €24 for three.

A **taxi** will take about the same time as the X95 bus and should cost €38 (day rate)–54 (night rate) from the airport to Sýndagma Square or environs.

B

BUDGETING FOR YOUR TRIP

These are some rough estimates for your main expenses:

Scheduled return flight from London: £120–£300 depending on season.

Scheduled flight from New York: $500–$1300 depending on season.

Hotel room in mid-range hotel in high season: €90–180 per night.

Meal in mid-range taverna with house wine (per person): €20–26.

Weekly car rental for a small car in high season: €260 unlimited mileage with a small local chain, €350 with a major international chain. In low season this range becomes €150–€250. Especially if you want to pick up your car at the airport, it's worth pre-booking a car online before your journey.

One-way hydrofoil/catamaran ticket to Égina: €14; to Póros: €25.50; to Ýdra: €30 (cheaper by ferry, not available for Ýdra).

C

CAR HIRE (see also Driving)

Athens is a very congested city with a critical (and expensive) parking situation; the main tourist attractions are concentrated in such a small area that it makes little sense to hire a car. Using public transport will limit the amount of walking you do, and taxis are plentiful and affordable. However, if you intend to spend a few days touring the Argolid or heading for Delphi, a car would definitely be an asset.

Those intending to hire a car should carry an International Driving Permit if from the US, the UK post-Brexit, Canada or Australia (national licences alone are not valid, and there are heavy fines if you're detected driving without an IDP). Alternatively, all European Economic Area national driver's licences are accepted, provided that they have been held for one full year and the driver is over 21 years of age (sometimes 23 years for certain agencies). You will also need a credit card for a deposit; debit cards are not accepted, though you may pay for the actual rental with those.

Many brochure rates seem attractive because they do not include personal insurance, collision damage waiver (CDW) or VAT at 24 percent. Most agencies have a waiver excess of between €450 and €700 – the amount you're responsible for if your vehicle gets smashed or stolen, even with CDW coverage. Your card will be blocked at the outset for this amount, which is released upon safe return of the car. It is strongly suggested you purchase extra cover (often called Super CDW or Liability Waiver Surcharge) to reduce this risk to zero; UK or North American residents can buy good-value annual policies from companies like Voyager (www.voyagerinsurance.com in UK, www.voyagerinsurance.net in the USA).

All the major international chains are represented in the arrivals concourse of the airport. In central Athens, almost all rental companies have offices at the start of Syngroú Avenue in Makrygiánni district, and comparison shopping for quotes a day or so before you need a car can be very productive. Some smaller but reputable agencies to try include:

Auto Union, Kallíróis 23, tel: 210 82 21 211, www.autounion.gr
Avance, Syngroú 40–42, tel: 210 92 00 100, www.avance.gr
Avanti, Syngroú 50, tel: 210 92 33 919 **Budget,** Syngroú 23, tel: 210 92 14 771, www.budget.com **Kosmos,** Syngroú 5, tel: 210 92 34 695, www.kosmos-car rental.com

I'd like to rent a car (tomorrow) for three days/a week
Tha íthela na nikiáso éna avtokínito (ávrio) giá tris méres/ mía evdomáda

CLIMATE

Athens has a surprising range of climatic conditions and temperatures. Most summer days feature dry, furnace-like heat. Many Athenians leave the city during this season, and if you can avoid it, don't visit between late June and mid-September. From early June until the end of September, the weather is hot during the day and warm in the evenings, with twelve to fifteen hours of sunshine per day. Between early October and late April, the weather can be quite changeable, with occasional wet and windy days. Snow occasionally falls in winter, but rain – including violent thunderstorms and flooding – is more common. Given global climate change, historical patterns are increasingly unreliable.

Average air temperatures:

	J	F	M	A	M	J	J	A	S	O	N	D
Max °C	12	12	16	19	25	32	44	38	29	23	20	15
Max °F	54	54	60	66	76	90	110	100	85	74	65	58
Min °C	2	7	8	11	16	19	23	23	19	16	11	8
Min °F	35	44	46	52	60	66	72	72	66	60	52	46

Average water temperatures (Piraeus and 'Athenian Riviera'):

	J	F	M	A	M	J	J	A	S	O	N	D
°C	14	14	13	15	18	22	25	25	24	22	18	16
°F	57	57	55	59	64	72	77	77	75	72	64	61

CLOTHING

From early June to late September, light, natural-fibre summer clothing should suffice – with perhaps a wrap for later in the evening. Even though you are in a city, take anti-sunburn precautions; hats, sunglasses, sunscreen and long, loose sleeves are a must in summer.

In spring and autumn, bring extra layers in case of a cold spell. In winter, bring a heavy coat or waterproof jacket, and a pocket umbrella, as Athens can suddenly get cold and wet. There are often pleasant days late or early in the year, so a layering system – i.e. a pullover/sweater plus a light shell jacket – as for spring or autumn works well.

If you intend to enter any of the churches in the city, you must be suitably dressed. No shorts for either sex, and women must have shoulders covered. Shorts on men are considered undignified in any season; though this rule is slowly relaxing, you'll still see Athenian men sweltering away in woollen slacks even during summer.

Comfortable, practical footwear is essential for touring archaeological sites. Marble steps and walkways are worn slippery with age; other surfaces are uneven, which can cause twisted ankles.

COMPLAINTS (see also Police)

If you have a complaint, first take it up with the management of the establishment concerned. If, however, you get no satisfaction then you can approach the Tourist Police (tel: 171; offices on Dimitrakopoúlou near corner Anastasíou Zínni, Koukáki district) whose English-speaking officers are specifically trained to deal with visitor-related problems – complaints about taxi drivers, shopkeepers, tour guides and the like. Theft or violent crime, however, must be taken up with the regular police.

CRIME AND SAFETY

Central Athens is generally safer than most north-European or American cities, but the impact of its prolonged economic crisis and laxly controlled immigration has meant that crimes against people and property have shown a sharp rise since 2014.

Organised gangs of pickpockets target new arrivals stepping off the airport bus at Sýndagma and are also particularly active in Monastiráki station. You know it's about to happen when several of them corral you in a metro car (new or old lines) and then press you against the wall, the better to relieve you of your pocket contents – at which they are very skilled. Heavily laden passengers coming from Piraeus should avoid this station, but switch to the tram at Fáliro.

If the worst happens, contact card issuers immediately – your cards will be used to obtain fraudulent cash advances within minutes at Sýndagma bureaux de change. You will, of course, have also stashed away a photocopy of your passport, as well as records of your card numbers (and the theft-reporting hotline) in a secure section of your luggage. Sadly, the police are unlikely to do anything on your behalf other than issue a report for you to use when making insurance claims. Go as soon as possible to the precinct in which the incident occurred – for Monastiráki it's in a narrow lane just east of Athinás Street.

Once settled in your hotel, leave valuables and cash surplus to daily requirements in the room safe. Leave nothing of value visible in parked cars, especially in Psyrrí, Gázi, Keramikós, Metaxourgío and Exárhia where break-ins are rife.

D

DRIVING

Road conditions. Athens' streets are often gridlocked, so on many occasions you can make better progress walking than driving. Drivers jostle for position, often running a changing (if not red) light, and park wherever they please. Keep on the alert whether you are driving or walking.

The centre of Athens, the so-called *daktýlios*, has alternate-day driving midweek. That is, vehicles with odd-numbered licence plates may enter the central zone on odd-numbered days, and even-numbered cars on even days – Monday to Thursday 7am to 8pm, Friday 7am to 3pm, from early September to mid-July. There are, however, numerous exemptions, including rental cars.

Most roads in the countryside have no verges or hard shoulders. This can cause problems if you need to leave the highway. If you get caught in a storm the road surface can become treacherously slippery, especially in May when oily olive-tree blossom is dropping; most roads being banked wrongly at curves aggravates this problem.

Rules and regulations. Traffic drives on the right and passes on the left, usually yielding to vehicles from the right (from the left on roundabouts) – though this is not always observed, and accident rates are high.

Fill the tank, please. **Óso párei, parakaló.**
My car has broken down **To avtokínito mou éhi halási**
There's been an accident/crash **Ehi gínei dystíhima/traharisma**

The speed limit on motorways is 120kmh (74mph), 90kmh (55mph) on undivided roads, and in built-up areas 50kmh (30mph) unless otherwise stated, although these are widely disregarded. Both speed limit and distance signs are in kilometres.

If you need help. If you have an accident or breakdown while on the road, put a red warning triangle some distance behind you to warn oncoming traffic. Always carry the telephone number of your rental office; they will advise you in case of difficulty. If you have an accident involving another vehicle, or injury to persons or stationary property, do not admit fault or move either car until the traffic police *(trohéa)* come out and prepare a report; a copy will be given to you to present to the rental agency. Almost all agencies subscribe to one of the nationwide emergency roadside services (ELPA, Express Service, Ellas Service, Intersalonica); make sure you are given the pertinent phone number.

E

ELECTRICITY

Electric current throughout Greece is 220 volts/50 cycles. Plugs are European continental double round-pin, either narrow (Type C) unearthed, or fat (Type F) earthed. North-American-to-continental and UK-to-continental adapter plugs are available from electrical shops. Don't bring strictly 120-

volt equipment – most modern hairdryers and shavers should have a dual voltage setting.

a transformer **énas metaskhimatistís**
an adapter **énas prosarmostís**

EMBASSIES AND CONSULATES

Australian Embassy & Consulate: Hatzigiánni Méxi 5, Level 2, 115 28 Ambelókipi; tel: 210 87 04 000, www.greece.embassy.gov.au

British Embassy & Consulate: Ploutárhou 1, 106 75 Athens; tel: 210 72 72 600, www.gov.uk/world/organisations/british-embassy-athens

Canadian Embassy: Ethnikís Andistáseos 48, 152 31 Halándri; tel: 210 72 73 400, www.international.gc.ca/country-pays/greece-grece

Irish Embassy: Vassiléos Konstandínou 7, 106 74 Athens; tel: 210 72 32 771, www.dfa.ie/irish-embassy/greece/.

South African Embassy & Consulate Kifissías 60, 151 25 Maroússi; tel: 210 61 06 645.

US Embassy & Consulate: Vassilísis Sofías 91, 115 21 Athens; tel: 210 72 12 951, www.gr.usembassy.gov

EMERGENCIES

Police emergency Tel: **100**
Tourist police Tel: **171**
Fire Tel: **199**
Ambulance Tel: **166**

G

GETTING THERE

By air. At present, Greece has two internationally active airlines. Aegean Airlines (www.aegeanair.com) has flights from London Heathrow and Manchester to Athens, and seasonally between Athens and Dublin. Sky Express (www.skyexpress.gr) offers daily services between Athens and Heathrow.

From the UK, British Airways (www.ba.com) offers daily direct services to Athens from London Heathrow and sometimes Gatwick; easyJet (www.easyjet.com) flies from London Gatwick and many other UK destinations. Jet2 (www.jet2.com) provides services for much of the year between many UK airports (including London Stansted)and Athens.

From Ireland, Aer Lingus (www.aerlingus.com) flies (May–Sept) from Dublin to Athens direct.

From North America, direct flights to Athens are provided only by Delta Airlines (www.delta.com) from JFK, Emirates (www.emirates.com) or United (www.united.com) from Newark, and seasonally from Chicago and Philadelphia by American Airlines.

From Australia and New Zealand there are only indirect flights; the most reliable providers are Qatar Airways (www.qatarairways.com) and Emirates (www.emirates.com).

By car. The all-overland route to Greece from western Europe goes via Austria, Hungary, Serbia and North Macedonia. Motorway conditions in Serbia are excellent; in North Macedonia much of the E75 is motorway, with the rest being upgraded. Alternatively, you can drive to the Italian ports of Venice, Ancona, Brindisi or Bari and take an overnight ferry to Igoumenítsa or Pátra on the Greek mainland. It is then a three-hour drive to Athens. Quality companies currently offering trans-Adriatic services between Italy and Greece include:

ANEK www.anek.gr

Minoan Lines www.minoan.gr

Superfast www.superfast.com

Ventouris www.ventouris.gr (from Bari only)

By rail. The train journey from the UK to Athens is expensive and takes up to three days; it is not possible to buy a through fare from the UK or Ireland to Greece in any case. Rail services from western Europe can link with the ferries at Ancona or Brindisi for onward sailing to Pátra and rail transfer to Athens. It only really makes sense to arrive by train if you're on a longer tour of many

European countries. If you're contemplating this journey, www.seat61.com/greece is an invaluable planning and booking resource.

GUIDES AND TOURS

Only officially certified guides may conduct tours of archaeological sites. You will find official guides at the entrance to the Acropolis, or you can book a personal guide through the nearby Greek National Tourist Organisation (EOT) office on Dionysíou Areopagítou.

There is ample choice if you want to book a guided group tour of Athens; however, walking tours are preferable to coach tours, which are likely to spend much of their time stalled in dense traffic. A coach tour is of most use for visiting Delphi, which is somewhat complicated to reach by public transport. Hotel reception desks are happy to arrange land tours for you, with pick-up/drop-off at the hotel.

Some of the most rewarding Athenian tours are special interest ones, such culinary/cooking tours, which delve below the surface of Greek cuisine with escorted shopping and tasting. Contact www.culinarybackstreets.com/culinary-walks/athens; www.secretfoodtours.com/athens; www.alternative athens.com; www.athens-walks.com; or www.athensurbanadventures.com.

Despite the horrendous traffic on the main avenues, cycle touring (especially if it takes in the nearby countryside) is also popular. Contact www.athens bybike.gr, www.athensbiketours.com or www.rollinathens.tours.

Heavily promoted 'three-islands-in-one-day' cruises of the Saronic Gulf are best avoided, allowing little time at each island. With a careful eye to hydrofoil or catamaran schedules, you can construct your own more leisurely itinerary taking in at least two islands.

H

HEALTH AND MEDICAL CARE

In case of medical emergency, **dial 166** (Greek) for an ambulance or to find the nearest open hospital. Emergency treatment is given free at public hospital casualty wards (ask for the thálamos epígonda peristatiká). EU residents can get further theoretically free treatment (in practice there are small 'appointment fees'), but must carry a European Health Insurance Card (EHIC; www.gov.uk/european-health-insurance-card to get one). Brits may now use a Global Health Insurance card for many of the same benefits; apply through www.nhs.uk. It is advisable to take out additional travel insurance to cover you for protracted private treatment or repatriation.

If you are taking any medication, bring enough for your holiday needs and keep it in its original packaging. If you have a basic medical need, look for a chemist, or *farmakío*, signified by a green cross, where you may obtain advice. Most pharmacists speak some English.

Athens tap water is safe to drink, though bottled spring water from Crete or the mainland mountains is universally available.

Where's the nearest (all-night) pharmacy? **Pou íne to kondinótero (dianikterévon) farmakío?**
I need a doctor/dentist **Hriázome éna giatró/odondogiatró**
an ambulance **éna asthenofóro**
a hospital **nosokomío**
I have... **Ého...**
a headache **ponokéfalo**
a fever **pyretós**
an upset stomach **anakatoméno stomáhi**
sunstroke **ilíasi**

L

LGBTQ+ TRAVELLERS

Greece is a very conservative country where traditional family relationships form the backbone of society. However, there is a natural courtesy towards visitors, and this combined with all the different types of international tourist makes Athens a good destination for gay and lesbian travellers. There are gay-friendly bars, cafés and restaurants in the districts of Makrigiánni (south of the

Acropolis), Gázi, Metaxourgío and Roúf (around Kerameikos) as well as Exárhia (near Omónia). Check LGBTQ+ events, news and locations at www.travelgay. com/destination/gay-greece/gay-attica/gay-athens.

LANGUAGE

Don't worry if you can't speak Greek. Most people working anywhere near the tourist industry will have a basic English vocabulary. In central Athens lots of tourist information (including taverna menus) is given in (often idiosyncratic) English – Roast Lamp, anyone? The table below lists Greek letters in upper- and lower-case forms, followed by the closest individual or combined letters in English.

A	**α**	a	as in *fa*ther
B	**β**	v	as in *v*eto
Γ	**γ**	g	as in *g*o, except sounds like y before e and i sounds, as in *y*es
Δ	**δ**	d	as in *th*en
E	**ε**	e	as in *g*et
Z	**ζ**	z	as in English
H	**η**	i	as in sk*i*
Θ	**θ**	th	as in *th*in
I	**ι**	il	as in sk*i*
K	**κ**	k	as in English
Λ	**λ**	l	as in English
M	**μ**	m	as in English
N	**ν**	n	as in English
Ξ	**ξ**	x	as in e*x*ercise
O	**ο**	o	as in *ro*ad
Π	**π**	p	as in English
P	**ρ**	r	as in English but rolled more
Σ	**σ/ς**	s	as in *kis*s, except sounds like z before m or g sounds

T	**τ**	t	as in English
Y	**υ**	y	as in *country*
Φ	**φ**	f	as in English
X	**χ**	h	as in Scottish *loch*
Ψ	**ψ**	ps	as in *tipsy*
Ω	**ω**	o	as in *bone*
AI	**αι**	ey	as in *they*
AY	**αυ**	av	as in *avant-garde*
EI	**ει**	i	as in *ski*
EY	**ευ**	ev	as in *ever*
OI	**οι**	i	as in *ski*
OY	**ου**	ou	as in *soup*
ΓΓ	**γγ**	ng	as in *longer*, always medial
ΓΚ	**γκ**	g	as in *gone* when initial
ΓΞ	**γξ**	nx	as in *anxious*, always medial
ΜΠ	**μπ**	b or mb	as in *beg* or *shambles*
NT	**ντ**	d or nd	as in *dog* or *under*

M

MAPS

The Greek Tourist Office produces an excellent folding street map to aid your exploration of central Athens and Piraeus. There is also a free, useful map of central Athens usually available in the airport arrivals concourse. You can of course use the map on your phone to navigate around Athens, but you'll need to make sure you have enough data (see Telephones).

MEDIA

Radio. Much the best Greek-music station (with occasional foreign music broadcasts) is ERa2 (Second Programme) at 103.7 FM.

Press. Numerous English-language newspapers (US and UK) are available at newsstands. Online-only daily English-language publications include www.ekathimerini.com and www.greekreporter.com. The only remaining print magazine in English, published twice yearly, is the very useful *Greece Is*, a freebie found in better hotel lobbies, and also online at www.greece-is.com.

MONEY

Currency. Greece uses the euro (€). Notes are denominated in 5, 10, 20, 50, 100, and 200 euros; coins in 1 and 2 euros and 1, 2, 5, 10, 20 and 50 cents (*leptá* in Greek). Notes of 100 and 200 euros are regarded with suspicion, as counterfeit, and can often only be broken down in banks.

Currency exchange. Most banks (Mon–Fri 8am–2pm) exchange foreign currency notes but charge a commission (usually 1–3 percent). The best bank at which to change foreign notes is the Bank of Greece, not to be confused with the National Bank of Greece; the central branch is at Panepistimíou 21, diagonally opposite the Academy. However, you may find that staff speak little or no English.

You can also change money at longer-hours bureaux de change around Sýndagma. Some advertise commission-free transactions, but exchange rates will be inferior to those of banks.

Automatic teller machines (ATMs). These are ubiquitous in central Athens, and the most convenient way to get euros.

I want to change some pounds/dollars. **Thélo na alláxo merikés líres/meriká dollária.**
How much commission do you take? **Póso promythia pérnete?**
Have you got a bank-card machine? **Éhete syskeví POS**
   (prounounced 'poss')

Credit/debit cards. Many hotels, car-hire companies, airline or ferry agencies and shops accept credit/debit cards, though they are no longer able to make an additional charge to cover their bank costs. Card use is heavily promoted by the government to help stamp out the black economy; quite unlikely-looking establishments, including most eateries, have the necessary technology.

Getting the best exchange rates. Maximise your currency exchange by using local ATMs, avoiding airport kiosks and researching exchange rates before your trip.

O

OPENING TIMES

Most shops open Mon, Wed and Sat 9am–2.30pm, closing at 2pm on Tue, Thu and Fri but open additionally 5.30–8.30pm. However, tourist shops – in Pláka especially – will stay open seven days a week from 9am–10.30pm. Supermarkets open 8am–9pm Mon–Fri, 8am–8pm Sat; a few work 10am–4pm Sun.

Museums and archaeological sites have unstable hours which may not match those given in the text; do not assume you can gain admission to any state-run museum or site except Wed–Mon 9am– 2.30pm. The last admission is usually twenty to thirty minutes before closing. If open on Tuesday, a public museum has shorter hours. Private museums have more flexibility.

P

POLICE (see also Complaints and Crime & safety)

Athens' regular police wear two-tone uniforms, with steel-blue slacks and caps and powder-blue shirts, with a steel-blue jacket added in winter – except when on anti-riot duty, when they look like any such armoured force the world over. **Tourist police** (contact details under 'Complaints') have an additional white band on the cap and a white belt. These officers can speak English and act as interpreters should your case need to involve the main police force.

Where's the nearest police station? **Pou íne to kondinótero astynomikó tmíma?**

POST OFFICES

Post offices (open 7.30am–2pm) have blue-and-yellow livery and are marked 'Elliniká Takhydromía' in Greek plus 'Hellenic Post' in English, with a stylised Hermes head as the logo. Stamps can be bought here and at substations (usually stationery shops). Post boxes are yellow for ordinary post and red for express. Allow four to seven days for postcards to Europe; nine to fourteen days for the rest of the world. Packages for non-EU countries should not be sealed until they have been checked by post office staff.

The most central post office in Athens, with additional afternoon and weekend hours, can be found at the corner of Sýndagma and Mitropóleos (Mon–Fri 7.30am–8.30pm, Sat 7.30am–2.45pm,).

Where's the (nearest) post office? **Pou íne to kondinótero tahydromío?**
A stamp for this letter/postcard, please. **Éna grammatósimo giaftó to grámma/giaftí tin kartpostál, parakaló.**
Express/registered **katepígon/sistiméno**

PUBLIC HOLIDAYS

National official holidays fall on the following dates:
1 January New Year's Day *(Protohroniá)*
6 January Epiphany *(Ta Ágia Theofánia)*
25 March Greek Independence/Annunciation *(Evangelismós)* Day
1 May May Day *(Protomagiá)*
15 August *Kímisis tis Theotókou (Dormition* of the Mother of God)
28 October National Ohi ('No') Day
25 December Christmas *(Hristoúgena)*
26 December *Sýnaxis tis Panagías* (Gathering of the Mother of God's Entourage)
Moveable dates. The most important holiday in the Greek Orthodox calendar is Greek Orthodox Easter, which in some years coincides with the 'Western' (i.e. Catholic/Protestant) Easter, and other years falls a week or two to either

side of it – in fact anything up to four weeks. It is advisable to check the Easter dates (easiest on www.5ko.free.fr/en/easter.php) before booking a spring holiday as all services, especially flights, experience disruption at this time.

Moveable dates relative to Easter Sunday, all of them official holidays except Ascension Day, are the first day of Lent (Clean Monday; 48 days before Easter), Good Friday, Easter Monday, the Ascension (*Análipsi*; 39 days after Easter) and Pentecost (Whit Monday, Agíou Pnévmatos; 50 days after Easter).

T

TELEPHONES

The international code for Greece is 30. Within Greece, all phone numbers have ten digits; fixed lines begin with 2, mobiles with 69, urban rate numbers with 8.

Foreign visitors with tri-band mobiles can roam on any Greek network, but charges (except for EU nationals, where roaming is free) remain extortionate. If you are staying more than a week or two, it makes sense to buy a local pay-as-you-go SIM. Your device must be registered at time of purchase, but the number remains valid for some months beyond each top-up; if you return to Greece next season, you will very likely be able to re-activate the number, which won't have been re-assigned.

TIME ZONES

Greece is two hours ahead of Greenwich Mean Time and observes Daylight Savings along with the rest of Europe (but not the USA), moving clocks one hour forward between the last Sunday in March and the last one in October. For North America, the difference is seven hours for Eastern Standard Time and ten hours for Pacific Standard Time (plus or minus an hour during those periods affected by Daylight Saving).

New York	London	**Athens**	Sydney	Auckland
5am	10am	**noon**	7pm	9pm

TIPPING

Service is notionally included in restaurant and bar bills although it is customary to leave up to ten percent of the bill in small change on the table (there's no way to add it to card payments). In the week before Easter and at Christmas, restaurants add an extra 'bonus' to the bill for the waiters; taxi drivers also get a mandatory bonus.

TOILETS

All major tourist attractions have good public facilities. Note that in many establishments toilet paper is still disposed of in the bin, not the toilet bowl, due to narrow drain-pipes or linkage to soak pits rather than mains sewage.

Where are the toilets? Pou íne ta apohoritíria?

TOURIST INFORMATION

The **Greek National Tourist Organisation**, or Ellinikós Organismós Tourismoú (EOT; www.visitgreece.gr), is responsible for producing and dispersing tourist information. For information before you travel to Greece, contact one of the following offices.

UK and Ireland: 4 Great Portland Street, 5th Floor East, London, W1W 8QJ; tel: (020) 7495 9300. **US and Canada:** 800 3rd Avenue, New York, NY 10022; tel: (212) 421 5777.

The **EOT information office** in Athens is conveniently sited in a purpose-built cabana at Dionysíou Areopagítou 18–20 (Mon–Sat 8am–9pm, Sun/hols 9am–6pm; earlier winter closure; Fri 9am–5pm, Sat 10am–4pm; tel: 210 33 10 529).

TRANSPORT

Metro and tram. The Athens metro is clean and fast, and generally the best way to get around. However, delays and cancellations are becoming the norm as rolling-stock and track maintenance is neglected. The old metro

(Line 1), called ISAP, runs from Piraeus to Kifisiá. Line 2 runs between Ellinikó to Peristéri. Line 3 runs between Agia Marina and Doukíssis Plakendías, with two special cars per hour, clearly marked, continuing beyond to the airport. Line 1 operates 5.30am–12.30am, lines 2 and 3 5.30am–12.30am on Sun–Thu, and until 2am on Fri–Sat.

The tramway (Sun–Thu 5.30am–1am, Fri–Sat until 2.30am) operates routes from Sýndagma down to Voúla and to Néo Fáliro's Peace and Friendship Stadium ('SEF' on electronic car displays), with a link between the latter two points at Fáliro. Metro and tram share the same website: www.stasy.gr.

Buses. An extensive bus network connects most places that the metro doesn't reach. Regular city buses run from 5am–midnight every fifteen to twenty minutes per route. They can be crowded, so for short journeys it may be easier to walk or get a taxi. Augmenting the blue-and-white buses are patterned electric trolley buses. Major stops have an overhead electronic board displaying remaining minutes until the next bus, and its route number; once on board, stops are announced in advance visually and also vocally.

Bus numbers beginning with 0 operate in central Athens; those beginning with 1 operate in the southern coastal suburbs as far as Vouliagméni; 2 to the south-central suburbs; 3 and 4 to southeastern and central Attica; 5 to Kifisiá and the northern suburbs; 6 and 7 to the northwest; 8 west towards Dáfni; 9 towards Piraeus. 'A' and 'B' buses go towards the northern and eastern suburbs. 'X' are express services with limited stops.

Fares, tickets and updates. A single ticket for a metro, bus or tram costs €1.40 and is valid for ninety minutes after validation, allowing transfers between the three systems. Three-day (€4.50) and five-day (€9) travel cards are available also. The best solution, however, is to buy a reloadable plastic ATH. ENA CARD (only at metro stations or the airport), which gives a sharp discount if you buy enough rides at once – e.g eleven for €13.50; unused journeys stay valid until your next visit. Get current information at www.athenacard.gr. The bus and trolley network itself is covered by www.oasa.gr; it's tricky to use but once you master it all you need to know is there. Can't or won't? Visit the OASA office at Metsóvou 15 in Exárhia (Mon–Fri 9am–2.15pm).

Tickets for metro, bus or tram are best purchased at metro stations, either from coin-op machines or an attended window. Fines for fare-dodging are a stiff sixty times the amount of the single fare evaded; rules are complicated, so unwitting violations occur. The main hazards for newcomers are attempting to switch from airport express bus to metro (not allowed) or forgetting to validate tickets.

Taxis. Taxis, painted yellow and with a TAXI sign atop the vehicle and on the side, are numerous and affordable. Meters are set to €1.29 at the start of each journey, with a minimum fare of €3.72; the '1' indicates regular fare, '2' indicates double tariff between midnight and 5am, or beyond urban areas. Taxi drivers routinely round up to the nearest euro. Tariff rules appear on a laminated sheet mounted on the dashboard. In the city you can hail taxis in the street, but extra-long or -short distances may be unpopular with drivers. All hotels will call a taxi for you for pick-up at reception. Fare-fiddling is not unknown, so the following sample '1' charges are useful: short hop across the centre, €5–8; city centre to Piraeus, €15; city centre to the airport by day, €38 including airport surcharge, tolls and baggage. Phoning for a taxi attracts a surcharge, and luggage in the boot costs €0.43 per item.

Ferries, catamarans, hydrofoils. Daily services operate to all nearby islands, from Piraeus to the Saronic Gulf and the Cyclades, and from Rafína or Lávrio to the Cyclades. With internet access, check the website of Blue Star Ferries (www.bluestarferries.om), which handles all sailings to Póros, Ýdra and Spétses. For Égina, the following alternatives are also available: Saronic Ferries (www.sf.gr), the Agios Nektarios (www.anes.gr) and Aegean Flying Dolphins (www.aegeanflyingdolphins.gr; also to Angístri).

V

VISAS AND ENTRY REQUIREMENTS

European Union (EU) citizens may enter Greece for an unlimited length of time. British citizens must have a valid passport; the 90-in-180-days rule as described below applies as a result of Brexit. Citizens of Ireland can enter with a valid identity card or passport. Citizens of the US, Canada, Australia and New

Zealand can stay for up to 90 days cumulative within any 180-day period upon production of a valid passport; no advance visas are needed, but extensions of the basic tourist stamp are almost impossible to obtain – you must leave the Schengen Zone for at least 90 days before re-entry. South African citizens require a Schengen Visa, obtained in advance at a Greek embassy or consulate. It is advisable to check visa and entry requirements in advance of your intended departure date to ensure compliance.

WEBSITES

Websites for useful organisations have been included throughout this guide; however, the following general websites are also helpful:

www.meteo.gr five-day advance forecasts, with a dozen reporting stations around Athens and Attikí

www.odysseus.culture.gr the Ministry of Culture home-page, describing all public museums, castles and archaeological sites; English option

www.athensguide.com the Athens page of Matt Barrett's acclaimed general Greek website

www.ferryhopper.com look up seagoing schedules to the Argo-Saronic or any other islands

YOUTH HOSTELS

The following are the better, most central hostels in Athens, but go to www.hostelworld.com for more choice:

Athens Backpackers, Makrí 12, www.backpackers.gr.

Student and Traveller's Inn, Kydathinéon 16, www.studenttravellersinn.com.

City Circus Athens, Sarri 16, Athina 105 53, www.citycircus.gr.

Athens Studios, Veikou 3, Athina 117 42, www.athensstudios.gr.

Zeus Hostel, Sofokleous 27, Athina 131 22, www.zeushostel.com.

WHERE TO STAY

Hotels are categorised by a star system, of zero to five in ascending order of luxury. Room rates for all categories other than five star/luxury are government-controlled. Categories are determined by the common facilities at the hotel, not by the quality of the rooms. Thus, a three-star hotel room may be just as comfortable as a five-star/luxury hotel room, but will not have access to a conference room, swimming pool and so on. All two-star hotels are en suite, clean and reasonably furnished, and should provide breakfast. One-star/D-class hotels must be en suite but will usually have little else on offer; no-star hotels are effectively extinct in Athens.

Tax and service charges should be included in quoted rates, though breakfast (typically €6–12 per person) may not be. The price ranges below are for a double room per night in high season.

€€€€	**above 300 euros**
€€€	**151–300 euros**
€€	**80–150 euros**
€	**below 80 euros**

MAKRYGIÁNNI AND VEÍKOU

Acropolis Select €€ *Falírou 37–39, 117 42 Athens, metro Syngrou-Fix, tel: 210 92 11 610, www.acropoliselect.gr.* A six-storey hotel with helpful staff and a reasonable location. It has a pleasant ground-floor lounge-bar, a plush breakfast area behind with skylight, affiliated parking down the street, and a rooftop restaurant (noon–midnight) with full-on views of Filopappou and the Acropolis. Some rooms also have Acropolis views. The single, cramped lift is a minus. 72 rooms.

Hera €€€ *Falírou 9, 117 42 Athens, metro Akropoli, tel: 210 923 6682, www.hera hotel.gr.* The Hera has perhaps the best roof garden in the area, with a heated bar-restaurant for all-year operation. Standard rooms are on the small side, so it's worth paying extra for three fifth-floor junior suites with bigger balconies (some fourth-floor rooms also have Acropolis views). The dome-lit atrium-breakfast room, and friendly staff, are further assets. 38 units.

Marble House € *Alley off Anastasíou Zínni 35, 117 41 Athens, metro Syngroú-Fix, tel: 210 92 28 294,* www.marblehouse.gr. This welcoming, family-run pension has an enviably quiet location. All rooms have balconies, baths, fridges, air con and free Wi-Fi. Great value – book well in advance. Sixteen rooms, plus an apartment fitting five. Credit cards accepted for deposit only.

PLÁKA

Acropolis House €–€€ *Kódrou 6–8, 105 57 Athens, metro Sýndagma, tel: 210 32 22 344,* www.acropolishouse.gr. The first Neoclassical mansion in Athens to be converted into a pension. The building's listed status prevents some of its rooms having en suite baths, though for the academic clientele that's part of the charm, and it is well kept. All rooms have solid wood floors, most have high ceilings (some with murals). Communal fridge and two breakfast rooms. Nineteen rooms include a few singles and family quads. Cash preferred.

Ava €€€–€€€€ *Lysikrátous 9–11, 105 58 Athens, tel: 210 32 59 000,* www.avahotel.gr. Suite-format hotel (three categories), thoroughly overhauled to the highest standards in 2016. Upper units have balconies with courtyard, or oblique Acropolis views. Roomier (up to 55 square metres) units, effectively one-bedroom apartments, comfortably fit a family of four. There are also smaller suites suitable for couples. Bathrooms often have a tub with rain shower overhead; kitchenettes are not meant for serious cooking, thus breakfast included in some rates. Wi-Fi throughout, assiduous service.

Electra Palace €€€–€€€€ *Navárhou Nikodímou 18–20 105 57 Athens, tel: 210 33 70 000,* www.electrahotels.gr. The only real luxury outfit in Pláka, the Neoclassical Electra Palace forms an oasis, with a small pool and pleasant spa in the basement, and a lawn-garden. Luxury suites have dark wood floors, antique rugs and Jacuzzis. A newer wing with a rooftop pool perches above the parking garage (fee). 155 units.

Phaedra € *Herefóndos 16, corner Adrianoú, 105 58 Athens, metró Acropolis, tel: 210 32 38 461,* www.hotelphaedra.com. The Phaedra, refurbished in 2019, offers the best budget value in Pláka. Not all rooms are en suite, but some have balconies looking onto the square around Agía Ekateríni Byzantine church. Breakfast is served in a pleasant ground-floor salon. The roof terrace has seating but as yet no bar. 21 rooms; one must book long in advance.

MONASTIRÁKI AND PSYRRÍ

Attalos €€ *Athinás 29, 105 54 Athens, metro Monastiráki, tel: 210 32 12 801,* www.attaloshotel.com. This friendly hotel offers good value and retains many period features, but medium-sized rooms (last redone 2017–18) themselves – about half with balconies, costing a tad more – have modern furnishings, double glazing against street noise, parquet floors and pastel/earth tones. Views vary – from internal airshafts to cityscapes. Facilities include a roof-terrace bar operating 4pm–midnight. 78 rooms, including some family quads.

Cecil € *Athinás 39, 105 54 Athens, tel: 210 32 17 079,* www.cecil.gr. This well-restored 1850s vintage mansion has some great period features such as its iron-cage elevator. For conservation reasons, rooms have no balconies – unless you count the ornamental ones out front – but they offer parquet floors, iron bedsteads, double glazing, pastel colours and retiled baths. Breakfast served on first floor. 39 rooms.

O & B Boutique Hotel €€–€€€ *Leokoríou 7, off Platía Asomáton, 105 54 Athens, metro Thisío, tel: 210 33 12 940,* www.oandbhotel.com. 'O & B' stands for 'ochre and brown', the dominant colours of both common areas and individual units. The pleasant ground-floor breakfast salon becomes an à la carte restaurant. Junior suite no. 22 has a big balcony and Acropolis view; standard doubles lack balconies. Total 22 rooms and suites in seven categories.

OMÓNIA

Fresh €€€ *Sofokléous 26, corner Klisthénous, 105 52 Athens, metro Omónia, tel: 210 52 48 511,* www.freshhotel.gr. Fresh completely rethought its original concept in 2019. Just a few of the original, lollipop-colour panels remain, in executive room 807 with its wood-effect flooring. Standard rooms have smaller balconies and no sofas. Hi-tech features throughout include bedside remote control of windows and plasma TV. The rooftop pool with adjacent Air-Lounge bar-restaurant is a big hit and all bathrooms are supplied with high-end Korres sundries. Free sauna and gym on the mezzanine level. 133 rooms.

Pallas Athena €€€–€€€€ *Athinás 65, 105 51 Athens, metro Omónia, tel: 210 32 50 900,* www.grecotelpallasathena.com. Now a member of the respected Grecotel chain, Pallas Athena's lobby has tables made of log slices, and slightly edgy wall art. The first-floor breakfast salon and restaurant (1–11pm), with indoor/outdoor tables, has more outré items, like a fake full-sized zebra. A small basement gym has two rooms full of machines and weights, but no natural light. 63 units, at least one adapted for guests with mobility issues.

SÝNDAGMA

Grande Bretagne €€€€ *Platía Syndágmatos, metro Sýndagma, tel: 210 33 30 000,* www.grandebretagne.gr. Perhaps the most famous hotel in Athens, oozing history and class (and never less than €872 per night!), the Grande Bretagne building on Sýndagma Square dates originally from 1846. Sumptuous communal areas include a landscaped outdoor pool garden, a ballroom, plus a basement spa with a palm court, and large pool, hammam and sauna. 320 rooms, with either city or courtyard view.

King George Palace €€€€ *Platía Syndágmatos, metro Sýndagma, tel: 210 32 22 210,* www.marriott.com. The King George Palace is a more intimate, scaled-down version of the Grande Bretagne. It has the same Second Empire furnishings, which jar a bit with the flat-screen TVs, recessed lighting and sound systems. Bathrooms are palatial, with marble trim and rain showers. Actively pitched at a business clientele, with four functions rooms, gym and spa. 102 rooms and suites, including a spectacular penthouse with private, Acropolis-view pool.

KOLONÁKI

St George Lycabettus €€€–€€€€ *Kleoménous 2, 106 75 Athens, metro Evangelismós, tel: 210 74 16 000,* www.sgl.gr. A 2016-renovated hotel at the foot of

Mount Lykavittós (Lycabettus). Room decor varies from plush to minimalist; all have Wi-Fi access, the most covetable overlook the city. Facilities include spa, gym and rooftop pool, as well as an in-house art gallery. 154 rooms, fifteen suites.

Periscope €€€ *Háritos 22, 106 75 Athens, metro Evangelismós, tel: 210 72 97 200*, www.yeshotels.gr/periscope. Design-led hotel with arresting dark brown-, beige-, blue- and grey-toned rooms; the higher you are in the building, the better the units, culminating in airy balconied suites, the penthouse having a private Jacuzzi. All units (superior doubles the norm) have pillow menus, Simmons-brand mattresses, wood floors, electric blackout curtains, flat-screen TVs and music systems, ingenious combination work desk/dressers, cityscapes projected onto the ceiling, and wet-rooms with walk-in rain showers. Junior suites, unlike doubles, all have proper balconies with table and chairs. Breakfast (in the ground-floor lounge, with its submarine video projection) is buffet format, plus cooked-to-order dishes. 22 units in four grades.

AMBELÓKIPI (PLATÍA MAVÍLI)

Alexandros €€–€€€ *Timoléondos Vássou 8, 115 21 Athens, metro Ambelókipi, tel: 210 64 30 464*, www.airotel.gr. On a little square behind a chapel, Alexandros (part of the Airotel chain) offers decent accommodation behind a slightly forbidding exterior. The high-ceilinged lounge is flanked by the white-brick-and-fabric-panelled restaurant, redone in 2018. The bar has a billiard table and computer/printer. Alexandros' real USP is its rooftop Urban Beach (www.mavilibeach.gr; May–Oct, open to all): real sea-sand with sunbeds or daybeds and a pool just to cool off in; the adjacent bistro-bar runs noon–11pm. 63 units, including many single rooms, and nineteen suites, mostly have big balconies, earth-tone fabric floor and papered walls; bathrooms feature rain and 'telephone' showers and big sinks. The senior suite lacks a balcony but has a king-size bed, deep blue carpeting, a sofa-bed for two kids, and two sinks in the bathroom. Free parking on site, 'by availability'.

Embassy €€ *Timoléondos Vássou 22, 115 21 Athens, metro Ambelókipi, tel: 210 64 15 000*, www.embassyhotel.gr. Businessmen's hotel with rooms sporting veneer floors and bathrooms with steel sinks, done up in blue, grey and white hues (except for junior suites in earth tones). Rear units have balconies with a leafy view, though front rooms are bigger, with round dining tables. All have trouser presses and coffee/tea machines. Common areas are restricted to the ground-floor bar and breakfast area. Fee parking adjacent. 22 rooms, nine suites.

ARGOLID PENINSULA

La Belle Hélène € *Main road, Mykínes 212 00 (Mycenae), tel: 27510 76225.* This 1862-built house retains its Victorian ambience – you can even sleep in the bed Heinrich Schliemann used during his excavations at Mycenae. Conservation rules mean shared bathrooms, but the hospitality is excellent. The guestbook has signatures of the famous (e.g. Agatha Christie, Allen Ginzburg, Lawrence Durrell, Virginia Woolf) and infamous Nazi leaders. 5 rooms. Cash only.

Byron €–€€ *Plátonos 2, Platía Agíou Spyridóna, tel: 27520 22351,* www.byronhotel.gr. This was Návplio's first (1986) boutique hotel installed in a restored old mansion, and following post-millennium renovation and expansion, is again among the best. Many units overlook the domes of a medieval hammam, and some have balconies. There are a range of rooms, mostly done up in warm pastel hues, scattered over two buildings – our favourite is the mid-priced one with solid-wood floor and pitched roof beams in the newer wing – for every taste and budget. Seventeen rooms. Open all year.

SARONIC GULF ISLANDS

Bratsera €€€€ *180 40 Ýdra (Hydra), tel: 22980 53971,* www.bratserahotel.com. This hotel occupies a former sponge factory, and the extensive common areas (including a conference room and Ýdra's only pool) double as a museum of the industry, with photos and artefacts. Large rooms, in eight grades, have flagstone floors and showers. Open late March–mid-Oct. 25 rooms.

Orloff €€€–€€€€ *Rafaliá 9, Platía Nikoláou Vótsi, 180 40 Ýdra (Hydra), tel: 22980 52564,* www.orloff.gr. Named after a Russian who fomented an unsuccessful Aegean revolt in 1770, this renovated mansion was one of the first boutique hotels on this island, and still one of the best. There is now an annexe of 'Legacy Suites' in a separate villa. The managing family is very helpful and can arrange restaurant bookings and special activities.

Brown €€ *Aktí Hatzí 3–4 (southern waterfront), past Panagítsa church, 180 10 Égina, tel: 22970 22271*, www.hotelbrown.gr. Égina town's top hotel, facing the southerly town beach plus the Argolid peninsula, occupying a former sponge factory dating from 1880. The best, calmest units are the rear garden bungalows; there are also galleried family suites sleeping four. 28 units in the main building, most with sea views, plus the bungalows.

Poseidonion Grand €€€–€€€€ *West of Dápia, on shore, Spétses tel: 22980 74553*, www.poseidonion.com. A 1914 landmark which, after years of neglect, has reopened as the island's top hotel. Choose between traditional units (seven suites, three types of doubles) in the original building or less characterful bungalows out back around the long, narrow freshwater pool. Main restaurant serves dinner only in summer, though the Library Brasserie is open 10.30am–12.30pm for late breakfast, then until 1am for snacks, while the outdoor Palms Bar is open all day until 10pm. Other amenities include a spa, gym, outdoor cinema (June–Oct) and on-site bicycle rental.

DELPHI AREA

Ganimede/Ganymidis €€ *Nikoláou Gourgoúri 20 (southwest market street), 330 52 Galaxídi, tel: 22650 41328*, www.ganimede.gr/en/homepage. This restoration hotel in a historic port south of Delphi is superbly managed by the Papalexis family. There are six doubles in the old ship-captain's mansion, remoter studios, and a family suite across the courtyard garden where a copious breakfast is served, featuring exquisite homemade pâtés and jams. Booking essential, especially weekends year-round.

Pan € *Pávlou ké Frederíkis 53, 330 54 Delfí, tel: 22650 82294*, www.panartemis. gr. Comfortable, excellent-value, friendly hotel with fine views of the Itéa gulf. Its *Artemis* annexe opposite has doubles equal in standard to the family quads of the Pan but lacking the sea views; a fireplace blazes there in winter. Thirty rooms total.

INDEX

Athens Transport

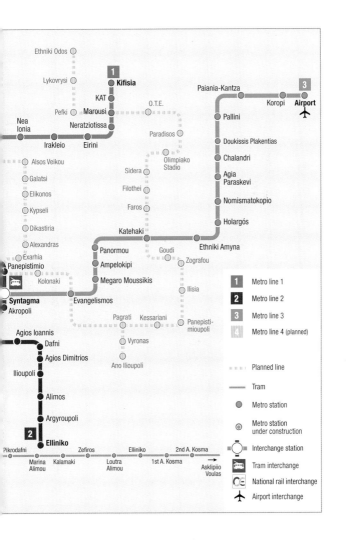

THE **MINI** ROUGH GUIDE TO
ATHENS

First Edition 2023

Editor: Lizzie Horrocks
Author: Marc Dubin
Picture Editor: Tom Smyth
Cartography Update: Carte
Layout: Greg Madejak
Head of DTP and Pre-Press: Rebeka Davies
Head of Publishing: Sarah Clark
Photography Credits: Britta Jaschinski/Apa
Publications 85; Daniella Nowitz/Apa Publications
5M, 5M, 15, 20, 66; Glyn Genin/Apa Publications
88; Greek National Tourism Organisation 5M, 82;
iStock 19, 33, 35, 36, 38, 42, 48, 61, 62, 73, 76, 79, 97;
Maria Kutrakova/Fotolia 30; Ming Tang-Evans/Apa
Publications 98; Public domain 17, 24; Rebecca
Bizonet 47; Rebecca Erol/Apa Publications 6T;
Richard Nowitz/Apa Publications 5T, 22, 56, 75;
Shutterstock 1, 4ML, 4TL, 5T, 5M, 6B, 7B, 7T, 11, 13,
28, 41, 45, 51, 53, 54, 58, 65, 69, 71, 80, 87, 90, 95,
101; Public domain 24
Cover Credits: The Parthenon **Tomas Marek/
Shutterstock**

Distribution

UK, Ireland and Europe: Apa Publications (UK)
Ltd; sales@roughguides.com
United States and Canada: Ingram Publisher
Services; ips@ingramcontent.com
Australia and New Zealand: Booktopia;
retailer@booktopia.com.au
Worldwide: Apa Publications (UK) Ltd;
sales@roughguides.com

**Special Sales, Content Licensing
and CoPublishing**
Rough Guides can be purchased in bulk
quantities at discounted prices. We can create
special editions, personalised jackets and
corporate imprints tailored to your needs.
sales@roughguides.com; http://roughguides.com

Printed in Czech Republic

This book was produced using **Typefi** automated
publishing software.

Contact us
Every effort has been made to provide accurate
information in this publication, but changes
are inevitable. The publisher cannot be held
responsible for any resulting loss, inconvenience
or injury sustained by any traveller as a result
of information or advice contained in the
guide. We would appreciate it if readers would
call our attention to any errors or outdated
information, or if you feel we've left something
out. Please send your comments with the subject
line "Rough Guide Mini Athens Update" to
mail@uk.roughguides.com.